T0304050

ROUTLEDGE LIBRARY EDITIONS: INDUSTRIAL RELATIONS

Volume 25

MANAGEMENT BY AGREEMENT

MANAGEMENT BY AGREEMENT

An Alternative to the
Industrial Relations Act

W.E.J. McCARTHY
AND
N.D. ELLIS

Routledge
Taylor & Francis Group

LONDON AND NEW YORK

First published in 1973 by Hutchinson & Co (Publishers) Ltd

This edition first published in 2025
by Routledge
4 Park Square, Milton Park, Abingdon, Oxon OX14 4RN

and by Routledge
605 Third Avenue, New York, NY 10158

Routledge is an imprint of the Taylor & Francis Group, an informa business

© 1973 W.E.J. McCarthy and N.D. Ellis

British Library Cataloguing in Publication Data
A catalogue record for this book is available from the British Library

ISBN: 978-1-032-81770-5 (Set)
ISBN: 978-1-032-81634-0 (Volume 25) (hbk)
ISBN: 978-1-032-81639-5 (Volume 25) (pbk)
ISBN: 978-1-003-50063-6 (Volume 25) (ebk)

DOI: 10.4324/9781003500636

Publisher's Note
The publisher has gone to great lengths to ensure the quality of this reprint but points out that some imperfections in the original copies may be apparent.

Disclaimer
The publisher has made every effort to trace copyright holders and would welcome correspondence from those they have been unable to trace.

Management by Agreement

an alternative to the Industrial Relations Act

W. E. J. McCarthy
and N. D. Ellis

HUTCHINSON OF LONDON

HUTCHINSON & CO *(Publishers)* LTD
3 Fitzroy Square, London W1

London Melbourne Sydney Auckland
Wellington Johannesburg Cape Town
and agencies throughout the world

First published 1973

*This book has been set in Baskerville type, printed in Great Britain by
Ebenezer Baylis and Son, Ltd, The Trinity Press, Worcester, and London
and bound by Wm. Brendon, Tiptree, Essex.*

ISBN 0 09 116570 9 (cased)
      09 116571 7 (paper)

In memory of Charles Delacourt
Smith – a great trade union leader
and an irreplaceable force for progress in the British Labour Movement.

Contents

Contents

Editorial Foreword

A combination of factors make it difficult for the practising manager or trade unionist to form a broad and forward view of modern industrial society and his or her role within it. Pressures of work and living, narrowing specialisations, the increasing role of external influences particularly from government, and the pace and diversity of change all conspire against such understanding. The expanding demands of specialised functions have affected education and intellectual activity generally, compartmentalising thought and knowledge and in particular tending to exclude social issues and values and to isolate industrial theory and practise from society in a dangerously unreal way.

Despite welcome developments in both the quantity and quality of education for industry perspectives are still blocked by the preconceptions of yesterday and the preoccupations of today. Even the younger manager attending a course has to make a considerable effort first to widen his view and then to integrate all that comes within it. The books in this series *Industry in Action* are designed to complement the individual efforts of those managers, trade unionists, students and others who wish to take this wider view. Within the framework set by the need to understand the complex forces which are re-shaping industry and society each book will impart the specialist knowledge and techniques relevant to its area of interest and seek to establish and explore the links between the specialism and the technological, social, political and other influences which are relevant to them.

In their book *Management by Agreement* Dr McCarthy and Dr Ellis illustrate the intentions of the entire series most admirably. Although the focus is on workshop industrial relations the authors make a powerful case for the view that 'management by agreement' can only be developed success-

Editorial Foreword

fully at that level within the framework of a broader agreement
as to how the economy as a whole shall be managed and with
what objectives. The reader can develop a perspective on the
problems of contemporary industrial relations with the help
of a lucid analysis of the alternative approaches adopted by the
policy makers in the past. As is to be expected when one of the
authors acted as Research Director to the Royal Commission
on Trade Unions and Employers Associations the approach
adopted leans towards the 'Donovan' view of the weaknesses
of the British system of industrial relations and the changes
required if a reform is to be successful. But weaknesses are
detected in the Royal Commission's analysis – which lead to
several detailed proposals for reform which go far beyond the
Donovan remedies. The weaknesses of the Industrial Relations
Act of 1972 is illustrated by reference to a range of problems
which it creates for managers and trade unionists and to
which – it is cogently argued – it offers no solutions. The pros
and cons of the reforms suggested by Dr McCarthy and Dr
Ellis are carefully examined and limits set to what may be
expected in the way of improvements in industrial relations
from their adoption. The authors have brought their extensive
practical experience and a scholarly approach to bear on the
central problem of British industry, and the results deserve
careful attention from all those concerned with its future.

K.J.W.A.

Preface

This book presents a view of what is wrong with the British system of industrial relations, and what needs to be done about it, that is not confined to its authors. Indeed in discussing the ideas it contains with managers, trade unionists, fellow academics and other interested parties over the last two years we have been surprised to find how often a wide measure of agreement has been revealed. Very often our views have been modified by this process. Sometimes new and valuable suggestions have been made to us and we have not hesitated to borrow them.

Yet because in industrial relations reform the details are almost everything, and the weight of the argument is what matters, we feel it would be wrong to list those who have helped in a preface of this kind. We hope they will regard this general but sincere note of gratitude as sufficient public acknowledgement.

There are, however, two more specific acknowledgements that we feel we must make here. The material in chapters Three and Four is based on a memorial lecture given by W. E. J. McCarthy, in honour of Geoffrey de N. Clark, Lecturer in Law at University College, London. His was a rare spirit, whose work and example influenced every serious student of our subject. The idea of developing the views expressed in the lecture into a book of this kind arose out of the discussions that followed. We are grateful for this stimulus.

We must also thank Dr Mark Freedland, Fellow of St John's College, Oxford, and University Lecturer in Labour Law, for his invaluable help and patience in undertaking to read our legal chapters. He has saved us from many errors and naïveties, but it must be made clear that we alone are responsible for any that remain.

W. E. J. MCCARTHY
N. D. ELLIS
Nuffield College

1. The argument of the book

'I would, as a last general exhortation, urge John Citizen
not to assume that the law is what he would like it to be. . . .
To pursue a false trail based on such a belief often leads to
disaster, for there are many real and assumed grievances for
which no legal relief can be given.'

RONALD RUBENSTEIN[1]

This book is about what is wrong with industrial relations in
Britain and what needs to be done about it. It is concerned with
the adequacy of various proposals for reform in this field, above
all the provisions of 1971 Industrial Relations Act. This is a
subject of continuing controversy and debate where it helps if
the protagonists make their own position clear from the start.
For this reason this chapter contains a brief summary of our
own main assumptions, contentions and proposals, which will
be argued at greater length in ensuing chapters.

We take the view that those responsible for the 1971 Act have
failed to observe Ronald Rubenstein's wise maxim that heads
this chapter. Their Act fails to recognise the legitimate and
effective limits of legal regulation in industrial relations,
partly because the law is not the instrument they would wish it
to be. Consequently, the institutions of the Act often pursue
false trails, chosen on mistaken assumptions, and this has already
led to a number of disasters. Most important of all, perhaps, the
Act has stimulated the pursuit of many real and assumed
grievances for which there is no legal relief. In the process it has
made these problems more difficult to resolve.

Yet much of the growing criticism directed at the British
system of industrial relations since the mid-fifties has been
justified. Quite predictably, it has led to the rediscovery of
certain traditional critiques of trade union behaviour first

developed in a coherent form in the nineteenth century, and included in the report of the first Royal Commission on Trade Unions in 1869. Such views stress the so-called 'overmastering strength' that unions have developed as a result of their existing legal immunities, and the 'irresponsible' use they are said to have made of their new-found power.

The line of these ideas runs through successive official inquiries and commissions to the present time. In particular, they permeated the Conservative Party's influential policy statement *Fair Deal at Work*, published in 1968, which made proposals in many ways similar to those first advanced by Sir William Erle and the majority of the 1869 Commissioners.[2] They concentrated on establishing new legal restrictions on union behaviour designed to produce what may be termed *bargaining restraint and responsible trade unionism*.

Yet there has always been available an alternative diagnosis and a quite different set of proposals. These can also be traced from 1869 through to the Report of the 1968 Royal Commission on Trade Unions and Employers' Associations (the Donovan Commission). In Donovan, and its forerunners, the emphasis shifts from overmastering and irresponsible use of union power towards concentration on the growing demands and expectations of workers as such, and the need to come to terms with them. Instead of assuming, as the traditionalist critique does, that the existing rules for managing conflict are essentially sound – if only unions would obey them – this second line of argument stresses the need to adapt such arrangements, especially joint procedures for dealing with grievances advanced by trade unions on behalf of their members. As a result this view allots a much more important role to management initiative and efficiency. So far as the law is given a role to play it is mainly seen as a way of promoting what we call *bargaining reform and efficient management*.

But these two views of industrial relations are essentially incompatible, and we think that the Donovan or reformist view is basically the right one. The trouble with the Industrial Relations Act is that it was written by those who accepted the traditionalist critique but were unable to ignore the Donovan

Report. They no longer believed that the rules were sound and wished to do what they could to reform them. Yet they remained convinced that the root of a great deal of the trouble lay in the irresponsible use of overmastering union power. As a result their Act consisted of fragments of the Donovan Report tacked on to a legal framework that was essentially derived from *Fair Deal at Work*. In some instances, for example in respect of how they propose to deal with the problem of unfair dismissal, this does not matter all that much. In the case of most of the Act's more important provisions, for example those dealing with industrial action, it matters a great deal.

The arguments advanced by the supporters of the Act are considered in relation to three of its most important provisions, i.e. the immunities granted trade unions involved in industrial action, the sections encouraging the spread of legally enforceable collective agreements, and the parts dealing with union security and the reform of bargaining structures. In each case it has been claimed that these proposals have both restraint and reformist functions. This is found to be most unlikely.

In so far as they have any lasting effect on industrial relations they will tend to intensify problems and to undermine moves towards Donovan-type reforms. The most that reformists could hope for is that in time they will become largely ineffective and dormant, although at the moment of writing this seems to be a sanguine view.

All this is not to say that the Donovan Commission said the last word on all our problems. What it did do was to focus on the right approach. It rejected the traditionalist critique, that unions should be confined in a legal framework impelling them to try to somehow 'manage' and 'contain' their members. It realised that membership of a union should be regarded as the essential gateway to participation in the management of industry. It also correctly identified the central problem now facing British management – the irreversible devolution of bargaining power to the shop floor. Moreover, it pointed to the most appropriate means of coming to terms with this development – namely the negotiation of more formal and comprehensive and forward-looking agreements.

But its analysis had three main defects. First, it thought in terms of a single once and for all solution and failed to stress the need for a continuous process of change and adaptation. Second, it did not go on to say how far this process would inevitably involve a sharing of managerial prerogatives and the introduction of what we term a system of *management by agreement*. Third, it had almost no proposals to deal with those disputes that are likely to continue under any system of industrial relations – however improved or reformed it may be. Indeed it had no positive suggestions for the immediate problems of industrial conflict at all.

We suggest ways of remedying these defects, and make a series of proposals that go beyond those advanced by the Donovan Commission. Our argument is that it is necessary to understand the pressures which we call *the challenge from below* and *the challenge from without*. The latter stems from the complex and rapidly changing social and economic pressures acting on most firms today. In isolation, these pressures might tend to produce a more authoritarian management style, as the number and range of necessary decisions increases. But because of the challenge from below management has to try to develop a more democratic and participative system of industrial relations. This is the fundamental lesson which management must learn, unions must encourage and the law should promote. What it requires, above all, is acceptance of the fact that today *no* area of management decision-taking is beyond the rightful concern of employees. In terms of collective bargaining this means that *any* subject is a fit one for the negotiating table. For only if management stops trying to defend what remains of the 'sacred garden' of prerogatives, will it have any chance of obtaining from the workers an appreciation and understanding of its own problems and limitations when facing the challenge from without.

What is needed is a form of collective bargaining which is open-ended, although conducted mainly by means of a series of fixed-term agreements. Its aim would be to search for ways of anticipating problems as a first step towards regulating them by agreement. In this way the emphasis would shift

4

from inquisitions into past grievances and claims, towards future initiatives and problems that need to be jointly solved. The resulting agreements would be jointly monitored, so as to form the basis for further negotiation and agreements. It is proposed that this kind of joint decision-taking might usefully be called *predictive bargaining*.

Predictive bargaining is probably the best method of promoting management by agreement, although it is not the only way. It is not, of course, a form of workers' control, but when combined with various other techniques and policies – such as job-restructuring, participation in promotion selection, and trade union representation at Board level – it can be regarded as a positive programme for effective worker participation in management.

But because it is no part of our argument that management by agreement assumes the disappearance of real and felt differences of interest between the different individuals and groups that make up the modern firm, we do not expect moves in this direction to result in the disappearance of industrial conflict. (Indeed, one of the attractions of the collective bargaining approach to workers' participation is precisely that it does not depend on such unreal assumptions.) This means that there will remain the problem of securing the best possible arrangements for dealing with those disputes and disagreements that always arise under any industrial relations system based on the continued existence of free trade unionism.

To bridge this gap, we propose a greatly extended use of third party techniques for dispute resolution (i.e., all forms of genuinely independent conciliation, inquiry and arbitration). This would do more to prevent and solve industrial disputes than all the legal restrictions on union action contained in the Act. For what are needed are alternative means of solving disputes, rather than restrictions on their means of expression which at best only exacerbate them or change their form.

The book ends with a series of practical proposals designed to give effect to policies of this kind, recognising that much depends on the readiness of individual managers to perceive the need for moves in the direction of management by

5

agreement, and much more on the willingness of trade union leaders to respond to them. Yet there is a crucial role for government, not least in providing support for a network of public agencies designed to encourage and assist the parties in their own initiatives. Adapting a term first employed by Professor Clark Kerr, we describe this function as one of *constructive mediation*.

Proposals are outlined for a range of independent agencies and services free from government control but financed through public funds, to promote the aims of constructive mediation, giving examples of how these services would work and arguing that many of the most intractable of present-day industrial relations problems, such as the recent disputes in the docks, might well have been avoided if they had existed in the past. There are schools of thought which question whether it is either practical or desirable to greatly extend the range of constructive mediation services – notably the objectors suggest that too much external intervention in industrial relations undermines the responsibility of the parties, or they make the often-heard complaint that too easy access to mediation, particularly arbitration, encourages inflation. These objections are groundless and essentially implausible.

But of course the responsibility of government does not end with providing the means to encourage moves in the direction of constructive mediation. One of our central themes is that reform can be greatly helped or hindered by the legal framework that either promotes or frustrates different kinds of bargaining behaviour. We therefore include proposals for a new industrial relations Act that promotes the aim of management by agreement, helps to make reasonable compromises more likely and is not rooted in mistaken assumptions about the role of trade unions in fomenting industrial conflict.

A final chapter summarises our positive proposals and discusses the link between industrial relations reform and the wider society in which it operates.

Notes

1 Ronald Rubenstein, *John Citizen and the Law*, Pelican, 1946.
2 Royal Commission on Trade Unions, Eleventh and Final Report, HMSO, 1869.

2. Alternative views of the problem

'... there exists something like an inverse correlation between the practical significance of legal sanctions and the degree to which industrial relations have reached a state of maturity. The legal aspect of those obligations on which labour management relations rest is, from a practical point of view, least important where industrial relations are developed most satisfactorily. There is perhaps no major country in the world in which the law has played a less significant role in the shaping of these relations than in Great Britain and in which today the law and the legal profession have less to do with labour relations. In the writer's opinion this is an indication that these relations are fundamentally healthy.'

OTTO KHAN-FREUND writing in 1953[1]

Two contrasting views of British industrial relations have emerged in recent years, each providing its own definitions of the problems of industrial relations, and its own set of proposals for their solution. Not only do these views contrast in terms of the analyses of the problems presented, they also conflict in the solutions they offer. (Chapter Three shows that the 1971 Industrial Relations Act represents an attempt to avoid choosing between these two views, and seeks instead to marry them together in a single piece of legislation.)

At the time when Otto Kahn-Freund expressed the view of British industrial relations quoted above, it was probably accepted for the most part by the representatives of both sides of industry, leading politicians of all major political parties, journalists, television commentators and most members of the public. This chapter is about how the view steadily lost ground in the face of growing awareness that something was wrong.

8

With the benefit of hindsight, we can say that Kahn-Freund's statement more or less coincided with the high watermark of a long period of relative satisfaction with our 'self-regulating' system of industrial relations; with its emphasis on industrial autonomy in which employers and unions were left alone to formulate their own codes of conduct, and their own machinery for enforcing them. Yet it was not long before this character-istically British approach to industrial relations confronted a growing number of critics.

Disenchantment began in earnest in the mid-fifties, and a number of factors were said to be responsible. First, it was revealed that the number of strikes was rising in many industries and firms, and that most of these strikes were both unofficial (i.e. not authorised by the union concerned) and un-constitutional (i.e. in breach of established collective agree-ments). Second, a variety of incidents took place within trade unions that received unfavourable publicity. They seemed to show that unions were abusing their power in relation to individual members or ex-members. Notable here were the legal cases of *Bonsor* v. *Musicians Union* and *Huntley* v. *Thornton*. Both involved refusals to work with individuals who were subsequently dismissed. More important still, in terms of publicity and critical public comment, was the case of ballot-rigging in the Electrical Trades Union associated with its Com-munist leadership. In the public mind at about the same time were the inter-union conflicts in the docks, and the much-publicised activities of the shop stewards' committee at Briggs Motor Bodies.

Third, evidence began to grow that Britain was not making the best possible use of its available manpower. In comparison to other countries, it was said, we had more than our share of so-called 'restrictive practices' operated by powerful work-groups in industries like printing and the docks, and in places like Covent Garden and Smithfield. A series of public inquiries and commissions criticised such customs and the alleged complacency of established trade union leadership in relation to them.

Finally, in the mid-fifties, public concern with the problem

9

of inflation continued to grow. An increasing number of economists and public commentators began to blame trade union wage demands for inflation, especially as a result of uncontrolled wage drift associated with local bargaining by shop stewards. It was said that unions used the weapon of the unconstitutional and unofficial strike to exploit the existence of full employment and distort established relationships between pay and effort.

Soon enough the representatives of official employers' organisations began reflecting this growing criticism. But they were not the first to resuscitate traditionalist critiques. These originated amongst two groups; first a number of leading journals and organs of opinion – most notably the *Economist*; second, as will be developed in more detail below, a group of Conservative lawyers and MPs. In both cases they returned to a critique of trade union practice and proposals for labour legislation that can be traced back to the views expressed in the Majority Report of the Erle Commission on Trade Unions of 1869.[2]

The essence of this critique is that while combination for trade union purposes should be allowed by law, if only to enable workers to balance the 'natural' power of employers, care must be taken to see that it does not lead to what is usually termed 'union licence and irresponsibility' that may harm either society as a whole or any of its individual citizens. From this view it is a short step to the advocacy of a special kind of trade unionism – usually termed 'voluntary' or 'responsible' trade unionism. On closer examination this appears to be a tame and harmless form of trade unionism.

To promote this kind of unionism, the Erle Commission urged a framework of legal incentives and penalties designed to remould existing trade union objectives and practice. Objectives they thought harmful, such as limitations on the number of apprentices or the closed shop, were to be made unlawful, as were various ways of securing lawful objectives, such as picketing or certain kinds of strike action. Only those unions prepared to show that their rules did not countenance such practices were to be allowed the protection of the law, and the device used to test whether they were willing was a form of 'registration'.

It will be obvious to anyone familiar with the present Industrial Relations Act that this view is reflected in many of its provisions. But because it is not a new one it seems reasonable to term it in the context of the present discussion the *traditional critique*. In this way we shall contrast this view with that expressed by another group of analysts and critics who were not represented on the 1869 Commission, but who have a relatively long history all the same. They are also represented in the Industrial Relations Act, but theirs is not the decisive view. Because it has so far found its most developed expression in the Report of the latest Royal Commission to consider these problems, the 1968 Donovan Commission, we shall term it the *Donovan critique*. At the moment our task is to trace in more detail the re-emergence of the traditional critique within the Conservative Party over the last fifteen years.

RECENT FORMULATIONS OF THE TRADITIONAL CRITIQUE

Three influential pamphlets serve to illustrate the reformulation and growth of the traditional critique within the Conservative Party. They are *A Giant's Strength* (1958),[3] *Trade Unions for Tomorrow* (1966),[4] and the most important and well known, *Fair Deal at Work* (1968).[5] There are some differences of emphasis between these three, but there is an important common theme.

All are dominated by a desire to find a way of reducing the general level of strikes, especially unofficial and unconstitutional strikes, which are viewed as particularly damaging to the economy because they generate perpetual uncertainty and disruption. Restrictive labour practices, caused or supported by trade unions, are also a common theme. Underlying the analysis of both problems is the conviction that they have little or nothing to do with established methods of resolving disputes in industry – i.e. present-day disputes, procedures and arrangements for dealing with workers' grievances or concerns, such as pay or job security. These three publications assume throughout that what may be termed the *rules* of the existing system are basically sound, and that the problem is to ensure that they are observed, especially by trade unions and their members.

Similarly, there is little acknowledgement in these three documents that problems may arise because management is authoritarian, or refuses to share its power. Once again the rules of the system, even where they are basically the unilateral decisions of management, are seen as being for the most part satisfactory. The trouble with workers is that they refuse to obey these rules, and even develop their own 'restrictive' rules in defiance of management.

Before analysing the arguments in more detail two preliminary points should be made. First, it is worth noting that nowadays their supporters invariably stress that the restrictions involved for trade unions ought also to apply, where possible, to employers' associations. (Thus we are told that employers' associations ought also to operate without the enforcement of 100 per cent membership via the closed shop.)[6] But it is important to realise that this argument is not as fair as it looks. The main reason for this is, of course, that employers' associations are not normally called upon to play the same role in relation to employers as trade unions are in relation to workers. Consequently the impact of their proposals fall much more heavily on trade unions than upon employers' associations. Certainly it is in relation to trade unions that they represent a major departure from existing practice.

Unions are required to give focus and voice to worker combination, which the traditionalists admit is justified to enable individual workers to match the 'natural' power of their employer. Workers cannot hope to replace individual bargaining by collective bargaining without the formation of influential and even powerful trade unions. Employers' associations are not necessary to employers in the same way. They are much more tangential organisations, resorted to as and when necessary when they appear to suit the interests of individual companies. Some systems of collective bargaining operate without *any* employers' associations in the British sense. Many employers do not believe that they need associations in order to come to terms with the unions they recognise. And the more limited functions of employers' associations are reflected in their rules and practices. By and large they do not wish and have no need to develop powers comparable to those of most developed trade unions.

Sometimes the traditionalists come near to admitting as much. They accept, albeit in passing, that their proposals relating to restrictions in legal status and changes in existing rules and practices are primarily intended to have an impact on unions. Thus in discussing their registration proposals the authors of *Fair Deal at Work* claim that:

> These conclusions apply both to employers' associations and trade unions; but in some respects they clearly have more relevance to the latter than the former – for example, the requirements for registration. This is inevitable. While most employers' associations are trade unions in the legal sense, the nature of their membership and activities is very different. Moreover, employers – both individually and collectively – already operate within a well-defined framework of law provided by the Companies Acts and the legislation dealing with monopolies and restrictive trade practices, for which there are no equivalents on the trade union side.[7]

Of course, the references above to the Companies Acts, and monopolies and restrictive trade practices legislation, are hardly relevant in this respect, if only because their main impact is designed to be felt outside the sphere of industrial relations. (In other words, in so far as they are effective management freedom is curtailed in its dealings with shareholders, or with customers and suppliers, rather than in its relationship with workers or trade unions.) Nevertheless, the quotation as a whole appears to justify our concentrating below on the impact of traditional proposals on trade unions.

A second preliminary consideration concerns the prominent

role played by lawyers in the re-emergence of the traditionalist critiques inside the contemporary Conservative Party. Both *A Giant's Strength* and *Trade Unions for Tomorrow* are heavily legalistic in tone and approach; the former was in fact produced by the Inns of Court Conservative and Unionist Society. *Fair Deal at Work* was written by a broader cross-section of Conservative politicians, including a subsequent Secretary of State for Employment, Robert Carr. Nevertheless, its arguments follow very closely the lines of the earlier publications, and its debt to *A Giant's Strength* is evident in every page.

Inevitably lawyers, like any other group of specialists, have their own preoccupations. In this case they begin with a concern for the observance of contracts and agreements, and a tendency to believe that observance can be ensured by legal means. This emphasis continues throughout subsequent publications and pronouncements of the traditionalist critique within the Conservative Party throughout the 1958–68 period. Thus, in spite of various qualifying statements paying lip-service to the notion that the law can only have a limited role in industrial relations, we find that until the publication of the Donovan Report, their policy proposals continue to be expressed almost exclusively in terms of new laws and regulations. It is only with the publication of the Royal Commission's Report that non-legal proposals find a place in the thinking of the new generation of traditionalists.

Turning to the arguments put forward in favour of the traditional critique in contemporary Conservative thinking, the most striking point is that the central defect of British industrial relations is seen largely in terms of the way trade unions have used past legal immunities. In the words of *A Giant's Strength*, the unusual degree of protection afforded to trade unions since 1906 has created 'the problem of restraining the overmighty subject so that his power is not used either intentionally or accidentally, as a means of oppression'.[8] This line of criticism holds that irresponsible and unofficial elements within the trade union movement, led and fomented by various extremist groups, have exploited an inadequate legal framework.

Criticism focuses in particular on the special legal protection for unions and workers provided by the 1906 Trade Disputes Act. This Act removed the risk of civil conspiracy for workers engaged in a trade dispute, and, most importantly, set aside the Taff Vale decision of the House of Lords which had made trade unions responsible for the wrongful acts of their officials or representatives. As a result it was clearly laid down that a civil action against a trade union 'should not be entertained by any court' unless the act complained of constituted a *breach of contract* on the part of the union itself. (This meant that while unions could be sued if they failed to pay their rent, or refused to honour legal contracts, they could not be made liable at law even if their officials or representatives were found to have induced an unlawful breach of contract in ways not covered by the 1906 Act.) Traditionalists argued that these immunities, coupled with the fact that most collective agreements in Britain were accepted to be non-legal documents, resulted in an excessive concentration of power within unions without sufficient accountability. As *Fair Deal at Work* put the point:

> 'Britain's industrial relations system is the least legally-regulated in the world, yet no other country has granted so much legal protection to the participants. Indeed, our Trade Union Acts give positive encouragement to practices which society would never tolerate in any other spheres of human relationships.'[9]

The traditionalist answer to this problem is to enact a comprehensive body of legislation designed to ensure that the power enjoyed by unions and their members is no longer exploited to the detriment of either the community or individual citizens. This is to be done in a number of ways:

1 The extent or ambit of existing immunities relating to strike action must be narrowed, so as to prevent strikes that are 'neither necessary to support legitimate claims nor desirable in the national interest'.[10] In *Fair Deal at Work* such strikes include 'sympathetic' strikes, inter-union disputes, strikes to enforce a 'closed' or 'union' shop and strikes called to prevent an employer employing certain

types of labour (e.g. dilutees) on work they are qualified to undertake.

2 Even where strikes for other purposes are involved, action must be taken to prevent irresponsible subversive or un-constitutional groups from leading, fomenting or 'inducing' such strikes, by restricting legal immunity to the 'authorised agents' of properly constituted and suitably 'registered' unions.

3 To encourage the leaders of such unions to do all they can to control any irresponsible or subversive groups that still exist in positions of authority within their organisation, the immunities granted to unions and union leaders under the 1906 Act must also be narrowed, so that in certain circumstances union funds are placed at risk where action is taken in the name of the union which involves a breach of the new and more narrowly drawn immunities (e.g. by shop stewards and others who are in some sense accredited union representatives).

As a further incentive to 'responsible' trade unionism, the traditional view also recommends that collective agreements should be legally binding. This means that the union could be made liable for damages if its members took industrial action in breach of an agreement signed on their behalf, unless it were shown that the union had taken all reasonable steps to prevent its occurrence. It is claimed that the additional legal penalties for strike action in breach of agreement will tend to strengthen the hand of 'responsible' union leadership, while discouraging less responsible union leaders from tolerating unofficial and unconstitutional action by their members. It is further proposed that the union should have the power, where damages are awarded against it, to take action against those members who have caused the breach of contract. The intention here is that the legally binding collective agreements should act as an additional legal prod (supplementing the risk of action in tort consequent upon the withdrawal of the legal privileges of the 1906 Act) to force union leaders to recognise and accept their responsibilities.

16

So much for the laws to prevent union power being used to the detriment of the community: what of the legislation required to prevent the 'Giant's strength' being improperly used against individual citizens? Here the traditionalists have focused on those features of trade unionism that seem to outsiders to exemplify undemocratic and anti-social attitudes towards other workers – namely the enforcement of the closed shop, inadequacies of union rule-books that permit unfair elections and other malpractices, and the effects on individuals of certain kinds of restrictive practices. The underlying theme is that these features of trade unionism have often been associated with the oppression of the individual unionist or non-unionist.

In the case of the closed shop, it is claimed that attempts to enforce it have led to unreasonable pressure being brought to bear upon individuals who wish to remain non-unionists, so that they have often been effectively denied the fundamental rights of freely choosing whether or not to join a union. Thus, although the principle of maximum membership of trade unions (and employers' associations) is accepted, there is the proviso that this is only acceptable so long as it is achieved by peaceful persuasion and discussion:

> ... we strongly rejected the concept that 100 per cent membership of either should be brought about by statute or by compulsion. No doubt the non-member can be a nuisance and is a complication. But his existence on either side of industry is the price of freedom ...[11]

The traditionalists' concern for the rights of the individual non-unionist means that they do not accept (and may not in fact comprehend) the *organisational* functions of the closed shop. They tend to see it as an expression of trade union prejudice and intolerance. The fact that the closed shop may be needed to enable a particular group to develop sufficient power to 'match' the natural power of the employer is not even discussed. The uses of the closed shop in helping unions to obtain and retain high levels of membership are not fully appreciated, while the dangers to collective action inherent in non-unionism are dismissed as mere 'nuisances' and 'complications'.

What the traditional view also rejects is the strongly held belief amongst trade unionists that there is a common obligation on the part of all workers who benefit from union action to take their full part in supporting this action once it is commonly agreed upon. In effect this is a version of the principle of 'majority rule' and the corollary that the minority should abide by the 'majority decision'. To opt out of an agreed decision – whether this involves resigning from the union or refusing to take part in strike action, or both – is in the eyes of most trade unionists to opt out of the system. We can compare this collectivist belief with the theory of democracy as it is applied to society as a whole, based on the principle that minorities should recognise the legitimacy of majority decisions democratically made. To opt out of the democratic system altogether, by either denying the legitimacy of such decisions or refusing to partake in future decisions, is to threaten the very basis of the system.

In the trade union context, collectivist ethics are not only founded on democratic principles applied to the needs of industrial action, they also have a strongly practical flavour. In many situations collective action can only work if the minority sticks to the agreed policy. Moreover, it is important to realise that for trade unionists, as for constitutionalists in other spheres, the fact that a decision has been reached by an agreed process for testing so-called 'majority opinion' legitimises that decision. Even where the majority of those qualified to vote actually abstain or do not bother to vote, as may often happen, what is important is that everybody should have the right to vote. Those who do not bother are expected to accept the policy adopted by what might be termed the 'recorded majority'. Otherwise, it is argued, decisions could not be reached speedily and effectively, which would make it difficult to take united collective action. Of course, in so far as the traditionalists realise this, their support of legal restrictions on the closed shop may still be justified: but then they should make explicit that preventing unions from operating closed shops is really a strategy to curtail their overall power.

The view that the traditionalist tends to take of union rule-books is that they are typically chaotic and archaic. The legal requirements for registration with the (former) Registrar of Friendly Societies are considered to be inadequate because they do not ensure that members can exercise reasonable democratic control in governing their unions or that there is adequate protection for the individual member against possible injustice at the hands of the union. Also, they do not prevent the inclusion of rules designed to harm the interests of work people who are not members or to restrict output and efficiency contrary to the public interest. Thus the traditional critique includes proposals for a new Registrar of Trade Unions and much more stringent conditions of registration.

These proposals concern the rules applying to the admission of members, the conduct of elections, finances, union officials and disciplinary powers. They aim to introduce a greater degree of public supervision over the internal affairs of unions in order to ensure that their rules do not conflict with the rights of the individual citizen or the public interest. In other words, the objective is to exert some measure of control through the law over those union activities which, it is said, have been traditionally carried on outside the law. By linking legal immunity from civil proceedings to registration, the two spheres of legal restrictions upon unions are meshed together. Thus, in order to retain some of their traditional legal immunities (although on a considerably reduced scale), unions are forced to subject themselves to the scrutiny of the Registrar.

THE ALTERNATIVE VIEW: THE DONOVAN REPORT AND ITS FORERUNNERS

When public concern has led to the establishment of public inquiries and commissions on the state of industrial relations, the traditionalist critique has usually been well represented. However, this view has never gained universal assent – even outside the ranks of trade unionism. Thus, in contrast to the traditionalist views of the majority of the 1869 Royal Commission, three of the members produced a dissenting Minority

Report. By 1894, when rising strikes produced another Royal Commission, the traditionalists were in a minority and the Majority Report advanced a quite different view of the problem with different kinds of proposals. In 1917, when the rising tide of industrial unrest prompted the government to set up yet another committee under the Speaker of the House of Commons, traditionalist views were again cast aside and the majority proposed solutions very much in line with the views of the majority in 1894. Moreover, when, in 1968, the Royal Commission on Trade Unions and Employers' Associations under the chairmanship of Lord Donovan produced its analysis of the state of industrial relations, traditionalist views and traditionalist proposals were once again set aside.

The Minority Report of 1869 was a rather unusual document, in that it made out the case for the maximum degree of legal protection for trade unions without admitting that there were any lasting problems of industrial relations that this would not deal with. On the whole, subsequent opponents of the traditionalist critique have not taken this simple view. Rather, their position has been that there are real problems – such as industrial unrest – but that these things could not be tackled by legal restrictions on so-called irresponsible and anti-social union power. Their view has been that the real difficulties, and the real challenge to the existing rule of law in industrial relations, derives from the growth of *worker* demands and aspirations and the inability of established institutions to deal with these adequately. As a result, the majority of the 1894 Commission, and the Whitley Committee of 1917, tended to look beyond legal remedies for their proffered solutions. Their argument was that what was really needed was improved agreements and arrangements between employers and unions for tackling shop-floor grievances and claims; in other words they looked towards rule reform, rather than rule enforcement.

This emphasis on the need for rule reform was a common theme in much of the more impressive evidence given to the Donovan Commission. Many unions, including the Engineers, the Draughtsmen, the General and Municipal Workers and the Transport and General Workers, focused on the need to improve dispute procedures at workplace and industry level. A number of individual employers, such as Richard O'Brien of Delta Metals, together with a handful of employers' associations, also pointed out the need to shift the focus of collective bargaining to the level of the plant or company. Several individual companies with experience of plant and company level productivity agreements explained how more formal bargaining at this level had helped them to deal with problems of wage drift and restrictive practices. Several industrial relations academics, in particular Allan Flanders, developed the case for more formal agreements.

But there can be no doubt that the Report of the Royal Commission did more than draw these ideas together into a convenient form. It established the most comprehensive case yet made for a radical approach to rule reform, which still represents the best short statement of the contemporary alternative to the traditionalist approach. For this reason we term this alternative view the Donovan critique.

It was perhaps the essence of this critique that it sought to demonstrate the relevance of its analysis by considering at length the very issues raised by traditionalists at the time, including the nature and extent of union power and its manifestation in so-called irresponsible and coercive practices. This is evident from the chapter headings of the Report, 'The Efficient Use of Manpower', 'Strikes and Other Industrial Action', 'The Enforcement of Collective Agreements', 'Safeguards for Individuals in Relation to Trade Unions', etc. Indeed, irrespective of the conclusions reached by the Commission, most of these issues are more fully dealt with in its Report than in policy documents such as *A Giant's Strength* and *Fair Deal at Work*. It is hardly surprising that the Commissioners took account of these issues. Not only were they affected by the ongoing debate outside, they also recognised that any solution which was not a legal one in the traditional sense would have to confront the issues already dominant in the public mind – e.g. the problem of rising strike incidence, the ineffective use of labour and inflationary wage drift.

Moreover, the members of the Commission did not wish to

deny the existence of these problems, together with many others that had given rise to the growing criticism of our so-called 'voluntary system'. Their point was that they arose out of the interaction between rising shop-floor expectations and inadequate procedures and arrangements for dealing with such developments.

The defects of existing bargaining arrangements, and their impact on the situation in many industries and firms, were analysed by means of the Commission's well-known description of the coexistence of 'two systems of collective bargaining' which were said to be 'in conflict with one another'. On the one hand, there was the 'formal system embodied in official institutions', characterised by the industry-wide agreement intended to regulate wages and conditions and arrangements for avoiding disputes throughout a given industry. This system was evolved in the belief that powerful national organisations on both sides (employers' associations and federations of trade unions) could deal with the problems of industrial relations in an effective and orderly manner. Unfortunately for this theory, an 'informal system', 'created by the actual behaviour of trade unions and employers' associations, of managers, shop stewards and workers', had evolved alongside this formal system, largely because its assumptions did not fit the realities of workplace industrial relations. The informal system was based on the recognition of the inevitable weakness of the central organisation in the face of the essential 'autonomy of managers in individual companies' and the irreversible growth in the 'power of industrial work groups'.

The difficulty was that neither the formal nor the informal system were designed to deal with this situation. The framework or 'structure' that the Commission thought would work can best be described by asking three related questions. One, what *levels* of management decision-taking was it intended to focus on? Two, what *groups* of workers was it intended to cover? Three, what *subjects* should be included in the new agreements?

On the question of levels, the Commission pointed to the inadequacies of existing industry-level agreements negotiated between employers' associations and full-time union officials, and argued for increased concentration at the level of individual plants or companies. It was because bargaining at these inter-mediate levels had been neglected that there had developed the ever widening gap between shop-floor reality and formal industry-wide agreements. Only agreements at the level of the individual company or plant could tackle the problems that resulted, by means of more effective wage structures, produc-tivity agreements, and the provision of improved procedures for avoiding strikes.

On the question of which groups or categories of workers should be covered by the new agreements, the Commission thought that the present structure of bargaining was ex-cessively 'fragmented' – especially at shop-floor level. It argued that much of this fragmentation could be reduced and even eliminated through negotiating plant and company agreements covering matters such as pay, redundancy and disciplinary questions on a comprehensive basis, thereby enabling common standards and criteria to be extended over wider bargaining units. Finally, on the question of what subjects should be covered by an agreement, the Commission favoured extending the scope of bargaining because it thought that many of the persistent problems of industrial relations – such as the under-utilisation of manpower – could be better dealt with if managements were willing to forgo some of their traditional prerogatives and were prepared to negotiate on new working arrangements and similar issues.

Two final points need to be stressed about the new frame-work proposed by the Commission. First, the Commission also favoured a move towards more *formalisation* in the bargaining process. It thought that agreements in this country were often too loose, or ambiguous, and that this could give rise to dis-agreement and dispute. Above all, it wanted to see more written agreements, especially within individual plants and companies. Secondly, the Commission wanted this more formal and extended system of plant and company agreements to be more consistent in its approach to such questions as wage relativities, work-loads, or disciplinary questions. Consistency was one of the reasons why formalisation was favoured. Both were thought of as ways of achieving more equity and order on the shop floor.

This emphasis on the inadequacies of existing rules provided the background against which the Commission went on to consider most other issues it thought it had to discuss – notably the demand for a new legal framework based upon the traditionalist view. Clearly the latter had an immediate relevance to the problem that most obviously dominated traditionalist opinion outside the Commission namely the problem of rising strike incidence. The Commission's answer was that the continued increase in the number of unconstitutional strikes in most British industries and firms since 1957 was largely the consequence of the very defects in existing bargaining structure that it sought to remove. As the Commission put the point:

> Unofficial strikes are above all the result of the inadequate conduct of industrial relations at company and plant level. They will persist so long as companies pay inadequate attention to their pay structures and personnel policies and the methods of negotiation adopted at the workplace remain in their present chaotic state. They will also persist so long as neither employers nor trade unions are willing adequately to recognise, define and control the part played by shop stewards in our collective bargaining system. They will continue until the confusion which so often surrounds the exercise by management of its 'rights' has been resolved by the settlement of clear rules and procedures which are accepted as fair and reasonable by all concerned. Our proposals for reforming the collective bargaining system are therefore fundamental to the solving of their problem also.[12]

The Commission would not accept that most strike action was fomented by irresponsible and subversive elements within the trade union movement, which the unions ought to be able to control if they were placed within the right legal framework. Therefore, it rejected virtually all the more common traditionalist proposals for a new legal framework – e.g. the removal of trade union immunity in tort, the ban on sympathetic strikes, the legal enforcement of collective agreements, and so on. Such a policy

> ... could be contemplated only if it was likely to result in a rapid diminution in the number of unofficial strikes. This however is not the case. The problem with which we have to deal is the readiness of work groups to take action without regard to the procedures of collective bargaining. This stems from causes which we have set out in Chapter 3. Among them any failures on the part of the unions to exercise discipline plays a very secondary part.[13]

Although

> ... the desire on the part of a minority to make trouble and the irresponsibility and weakness of others are factors which contribute to the frequency of unofficial strikes. But this is not the root of the evil.[14]

On the question of how to promote the most effective use of labour the Commission again came down against the traditionalist view. So-called labour 'restrictive practices' could not be eliminated by making them unlawful, or creating an equivalent of the Restrictive Trade Practices Court, which would summon trade union leaders before it and ask them to justify what their members were doing. The problem had to be tackled by reforming the rules. As the Commission pointed out:

> ... the formal system of industrial relations in Britain is especially ill-fitted to accomplish improvements in the use of manpower. Where restrictions are enforced on the workers' side of industry, this usually rests with work groups rather than with their unions. The formal system provides for negotiation between unions and employers at industry level, but these negotiations can rarely exercise effective control over the methods of work employed in individual factories.[15]

and again the solution lies in the reform of collective bargaining:

Our proposals for the reform of the collective bargaining system are therefore fundamental to the improved use of manpower. They will get rid of assumptions and attitudes to collective bargaining which have allowed restrictive labour practices to grow and efficiency to languish. They will put in management's hand an instrument – the factory agreement – which, properly used, can contribute to much higher productivity.[16]

It is, of course, possible to argue that the Commission failed to establish such a clear link between its proposals and the problem of wage drift and inflation. Nevertheless, there was a logical connection, and it needs to be mentioned briefly at this point. In the first place the Commission suggested that 'properly negotiated factory and company agreements' would, 'if widely resorted to', provide management and unions with a more effective mechanism for bringing wage drift and fractional bargaining under a measure of control – if the two sides wanted this to happen. Secondly, if the parties did not use their opportunities in this way, the very existence of effective negotiations at this level would, at the very least, make it possible for the government itself to plan more effective action. For 'incomes policy must continue a lame and halting exercise so long as it consists in the planning of industry-wide agreements most of which exercise an inadequate control over pay.'[17]

In rejecting the arguments for legal rule enforcement and trade union bargaining restraint the Commission was faced with the need to discover ways and means for hastening forward its own plans for rule reform. It is here that it broke most notably with the traditionalist critique. Its position was that if rule reform was needed the major initiative required had to come from management rather than unions. The Commissioners emphasised their conviction in the following way:

... if the basis of British industrial relations is to become the factory agreement, the change must be accomplished by boards of directors of companies. The Commission recommends that boards of companies should review industrial relations within their undertakings, with six objectives in mind: to develop comprehensive and authoritative collective bargaining machinery; to develop joint procedures for the rapid and equitable settlement of grievances in a manner consistent with relevant collective agreements; to conclude agreements regulating the position of shop stewards; to conclude agreements covering the handling of redundancy; to adopt effective rules and procedures governing disciplinary matters; and to ensure regular joint discussion of measures to promote safety at work.[18]

The emphasis was to be placed on 'voluntary reforms' in these directions and the role of the law was said to be limited to providing an institutional and legal framework that helped rather than hindered. Since the focus was to be on moving management the Commission favoured an Industrial Relations Act which would oblige companies above a certain minimum size to register their collective agreements with the Department of Employment. In its view registration would serve to emphasise that the responsibilities of management for the conduct of industrial relations lie with the board of directors, and also 'those aspects of industrial relations which . . . the public interest requires should be covered wherever possible by clear and firm company and factory agreements'.[19]

To move management along the road towards more efficient collective bargaining, a Commission on Industrial Relations was also suggested, bringing together independent experts from both sides of industry and elsewhere. It would investigate and report on cases and problems arising from the registration of agreements referred to it by the Department of Employment. It was envisaged that this body should deal with a wide range of procedural issues, including questions about the recognition of trade unions and the inadequacy of existing agreements.

Because of the Commission's emphasis on rule reform, and the responsibility of management for initiating this process, it has been suggested that it had little to say about trade union responsibilities to respond to such initiatives, that it was, in a sense, 'too easy on the unions' in this respect. This may be a valid criticism, but it is important to stress that the Commission took this view because it believed that in the past critics of the British system of industrial relations had over-emphasised the role of unions in general, and trade union leaders in particular, in bringing about, or failing to prevent, unconstitutional strikes and other problems. Its role, as the Commission saw it, was to stress the other side of the coin.

Nor did the Commission ignore the second part of the traditionalist case against trade unions, which related to their behaviour towards the individual worker. On the question of the abuse of closed-shop powers, and other issues relating to undemocratic practices, the Commission concluded that its research studies and other investigations did not justify the belief that there was widespread abuse by trade unions of their powers *vis-à-vis* the individual. However, the Commission did see a need for certain safeguards to reduce the likelihood of such abuses. To this end it recommended that a statutory procedure should be established to enable an individual to lodge a complaint if he considered that he had been unjustly refused membership or unjustly disciplined by his union, or if he believed that there had been election malpractices. It also recommended that the requirements of registration concerning trade union rules should be revised in order to provide better safeguards for individual members.

The nub of the difference between the Commission and the traditionalists can be simply stated. First, unlike the traditionalists, the Commission accepted the functional case for the closed shop. It thought it helped to promote effective and stable union membership, which was essential to the successful introduction of their type of bargaining reforms. It wanted to civilise the operation of the closed shop, rather than abolish it in the interests of abstract individual liberty, or to help weaken the giant's strength. Thus it was prepared to agree to a procedure to help the genuine conscientious objector – but not at the price of strong trade unionism. Second, in internal union government, the Commission was primarily interested in assisting trade unions to erect their own framework of self-governing rules. For this purpose it also proposed a procedure of registration – which it intended to make compulsory. But this procedure was not seen as a back-door method for controlling or limiting union action in the field of collective bargaining. Most important of all, the extra degree of legal regulation which the Commission accepted as necessary to deal with these problems was to be seen against the background of a Report which contained a range of proposals that were intentionally designed to promote the cause of unions and individual workers.

These included, amongst others, proposals to provide for an effective legal remedy for individual workers against certain types of 'unfair dismissal', provisions for legal pressure to be placed on reluctant employers to get them to recognise *bona fide* trade unions, suggestions for remedying certain problems rising out of the interpretation which the courts had placed on the 1906 Trade Disputes Act, and a number of other minor issues. Few traditionalist proposals dealt with many of these questions. None set out to provide an overall solution of them in a way that was as comprehensive as the Donovan Commission's proposals.

THE ESSENCE OF THE CONTRAST

The main difference between the traditionalist critique and the Donovan critique may be summarised in this way; first, neither side seeks to deny that problems exist and something needs to be done about them – indeed there is a remarkable degree of agreement as to the features of the British industrial relations system they set out to remedy. The contrast lies in the diagnosis of their cause and in the solutions deriving from this. Traditionalists at base blame trade unions for most of our troubles. As a result they quite naturally seek to reduce their power and influence. Supporters of the Donovan approach claim that this is a mistaken view of the problem. They believe that an extended and more influential trade union movement is essential for the good conduct of industrial relations. What is wrong is not trade unionism as such, or even the abuse of trade union power, but the inadequacy of established institutions, especially defective bargaining institutions which are unable to cope with the legitimate growth of shop-floor demands.

As a result of their diagnosis, traditionalists see little wrong with established rules and want only to see them enforced. This leads them to advocate a new legal framework of incentives and penalties. Above all they wish to put pressure on union leaders to force them to adopt a more restrained and 'responsible' approach. Those who take the Donovan view say that this is a profoundly mistaken proposal which cannot hope to get to 'the root of the problem'. What is required is not an attempt to turn union leaders into industrial policemen but a new set of bargaining agreements within which they can operate more effectively. Here the key role must be played by management – especially top management at plant and company level.

Because of their diagnosis of the problem, Donovan supporters rely far less on law than the traditionalists. Public action is needed, but it should take the form of a wide-ranging institution for promoting rule reform. In so far as legal prods are required they should be directed at the right level of management.

Those who take the Donovan view also dissent from the traditionalist analysis of the misuse of the 'giant's strength' in relation to individual workers. They accept the functional case for the closed shop and do not wish to use the registration process as a way of restricting union power. There is a case for new legal safeguards to deal with isolated instances of injustice, but this should be done against the background of a range of other proposals designed to deal with a number of long-standing union grievances and to advance union influence.

The reader might be forgiven for assuming that these two approaches are poles apart, and largely incompatible with one another. The next chapter argues that the 1971 Industrial Relations Act cannot be fully understood unless one sees it as an attempt to avoid choosing between them.

Notes

1 O. Kahn-Freund, 'Legal Framework' in A. Flanders and H. A. Clegg (Eds), *The System of Industrial Relations*, Blackwell, 1953, p. 43.
2 Royal Commission on Trade Unions, Eleventh and Final Report, HMSO, 1869.
3 *A Giant's Strength*, Inns of Court Conservative and Unionist Society, 1958.
4 *Trade Unions for Tomorrow:* The Memorandum of Evidence presented to the Royal Commission on Trade Unions and Employers' Associations by the Inns of Court Conservative and Unionist Society, Conservative Political Centre, 1966.
5 *Fair Deal at Work*, Conservative Political Centre, 1968.
6 *Trade Unions for Tomorrow*, p. 9.
7 *Fair Deal at Work*, p. 18.
8 *A Giant's Strength*, p. 14.
9 *Fair Deal at Work*, p. 16.
10 *Fair Deal at Work*, p. 30.
11 *Trade Unions for Tomorrow*, p. 9.
12 Report of the Donovan Commission, p. 120.
13 Ibid., p. 130.
14 Ibid., p. 127.
15 Ibid., p. 79.
16 Ibid., p. 85.
17 Ibid., p. 53.
18 Ibid., p. 263.
19 Ibid., p. 47.

3. The case for the Act

'We are not attempting to replace the voluntary system but seeking to reform and strengthen it.'

ROBERT CARR, 25 May 1971[1]

'People are fond of suggesting that this approach is in direct contrast with that commended by the Donovan Commission. The TUC in its document *Reason* has actually said that the Government has "casually cast aside an agreed report" and embarked upon an ill-considered doctrinaire frolic of their own. Nothing could be further from the truth.'

'I should judge that the major part of the Government's proposals are directly in line with Donovan recommendations.'

SIR GEOFFREY HOWE, 21 November 1970[2]

When the Donovan Report was published in June 1968, its analysis of Britain's two conflicting systems of industrial relations was well received. Politicians of all parties, leading commentators and the spokesmen of both sides of industry welcomed its proposals for more formal agreements focused on the plant or company. From that moment received wisdom embraced the general case for bargaining reform. Since that time hardly anyone has wished to suggest that *all* that is required in Britain is rule observance by means of legal enforcement.

It was much the same with the Commission's criticism of top management. It rapidly became conventional wisdom to suggest that part of the trouble was that management in this country does not 'take industrial relations seriously'. The idea of a registration procedure, and a Commission on Industrial Relations to follow up agreements so registered and to put pressure

32

on management to initiate reforms, secured widespread acceptance. For the most part the proposals of the Commission which
were directed at increasing the scope of individual workers'
rights against management – for example, in relation to unfair
dismissal – were also generally welcomed. Again it was com-
monplace to suggest that these were 'worthwhile reforms' that
ought to be introduced without delay.

For a time it even appeared as if the Commission's conclusions
concerning the role and functions of shop stewards and other
work-group leaders had made a lasting impact in traditional
circles. The Commission's research studies led it to conclude
that stewards were, if anything, less militant than their members and more of a lubricant than an irritant on the shop floor.[3]
These views were quoted with approval in the most unexpected
places, and the Commission's suggestion that it would help if
most firms extended and formalised shop steward facilities was
also supported.*

However, it became increasingly clear that the traditionalist
critique had been contained rather than defeated. A number of
commentators pointed to the fact that the Donovan Commission
itself contained several minority 'notes of dissent' in which a few
of those who signed its main report expressed their own continued addiction to certain kinds of traditionalist solutions.
Others challenged how far the Commission had really done
justice to traditionalist arguments – especially those concerned
with the need to do something about the state of the law in
relation to unconstitutional and unofficial strike action. It was
pointed out that the Commission really had no immediate proposals for dealing with strikes at all. It tended to argue that until
collective bargaining was reformed nothing could be done. On
both sides of the House of Commons the view began to develop
that this was a hard and uncompromising doctrine, which
would be unacceptable to large areas of public opinion.

Moreover, the careful analysis of the Commission as filtered
through the inevitable simplifications of the mass media,

* It is only fair to point out that the *Economist* remained a staunch and reliable
exception to all this. It continued to preach undiluted traditionalism throughout
this period.

appeared to many to constitute little more than a 'whitewash' job for trade unions. Surely, it was argued, trade unions *must* be responsible for some of the trouble in industry – why was it that the Commission proposed nothing that they found disagreeable? In fact this criticism was ill-founded, in that Donovan made a number of proposals in the field of inter-union relations which unions were likely to resist. Nevertheless, the idea grew that Donovan was right in much that it said, but that it was 'not prepared to be as tough with the unions as it was with management'. Ideas like this naturally paved the way for the reappearance of a more sophisticated and suitably modified form of traditionalism.

To many these ideas appeared to receive some support in the Labour government's proposals for implementing the Donovan Report contained in the White Paper *In Place of Strife*. This document followed Donovan in almost everything it proposed and did not suggest any reduction in the degree of protection granted to unions and their members in the context of a trade dispute. (Indeed in the case of breach of commercial contracts the government went beyond the proposals of the Commission.) However, it did suggest three new proposals of a more controversial kind that had been specifically rejected by the Royal Commission – the so-called 'penal clauses'.

The least controversial of these involved a threat of fines against unions who refused to accept a decision of the CIR in a recognition dispute. Much more significant were those suggesting the introduction of a compulsory 'conciliation pause' and 'strike ballot' to help deal with large-scale unconstitutional strikes. Since proposals of this sort had figured prominently in suggestions made to the Commission by bodies like the Inns of Court Conservative and Unionist Society they were understandably regarded as traditionalist in origin. And when they were dropped, as a result of TUC pressure, traditionalists naturally charged the government with a 'sell-out to the unions'.

Understandably enough, in the Conservative Party, events of this kind were used by committed traditionalists to argue against those who implied that Donovan had outdated their entire approach. In this aim they were greatly helped by the fact that

Fair Deal at Work was published just a few months before the Donovan Report – and that it had been enthusiastically welcomed at the time by the party leadership. Consequently, when the Conservatives won the election of 1970, it was perhaps inevitable that their proposals for dealing with the problems should take a hybrid form. Their 'Consultative Document' on industrial relations reform set out to achieve the best of both worlds as they saw them: rule observance *and* rule reform, union bargaining restraint *and* efficient management. The aim of this chapter and the next is to examine how well they have succeeded in reconciling these aims in the 1971 Act.

There are, of course, many parts of the Act that may be said in Sir Geoffrey Howe's words, to be 'directly in line with Donovan recommendations' – though they seldom go as far as the Commission suggested. These include the provisions relating to unfair dismissal and some aspects of what is enacted in respect of contracts of employment. It is also obvious that the Act is written by men who, in Robert Carr's words 'are not attempting to replace the voluntary system but seeking to reform and strengthen it'. This presumably is why the preamble of the Act accepts the 'principle of collective bargaining freely conducted', and why it contains various measures designed to promote this principle. It also explains the continuance by the government of the Commission on Industrial Relations, established by the previous Labour government, and the inclusion in the Act of Section 121, which provides for all kinds of 'voluntary' procedure references on Donovan lines. Most significant of all, perhaps, the Act does contain a diluted version of the Donovan proposals for the compulsory registration of agreements – although they are not to be brought into effect immediately.

On the other hand, nobody would dispute that there are some parts of the Act for which even its authors would not claim any reformist intentions. They are rooted firmly in simple traditionalist assumptions and belief in bargaining restraint. The most notable are those designed to provide the government with an additional way of preventing strikes which they regard as constituting a national emergency. That is those strikes which, in their opinion, are likely to be 'gravely injurious to the national economy, to imperil national security or to create a serious risk of public disorder, or to endanger the lives of a substantial number of persons, or expose a substantial number of persons to serious risk of disease or personal injury' (Section 138(2)). The same is the case, presumably, with those parts of the Act that seek to restrict the right to picket.

Much more interesting, and in our view more significant, are the remaining provisions of the Act, which have been presented in ways that make it possible to argue that traditionalist and Donovan objectives are being reconciled. In a book of this length it is not possible to examine all of them in detail. In what follows we shall concentrate on the three most important. They are:

1 The extent of the immunities granted in the Act for trade unions involved in an industrial dispute.
2 The sections in the Act designed to encourage the spread of legally enforceable collective agreements.
3 The provisions dealing with union security and the reform of bargaining structures.

Our argument is that under one or another of these three headings one can discuss the essence of the government's attempt to accommodate its earlier traditionalist thinking with the reformist aims of the Donovan Commission. And if, in these three crucial policy areas, a case can be made out for suggesting that the Act successfully combines the two approaches set out in Chapter Two, then Sir Geoffrey Howe can justly rebuke the TUC for implying that the government 'casually cast aside an agreed report' in the name of an 'ill-considered, doctrinaire frolic'.

The supporters of the Act can rightly claim that its authors have considerable ingenuity and enviable political skill. They might even assert on their behalf that the Act has improved considerably on the Donovan Report, if only because it has found a way to avoid the hard choice the Commission posed between reform and restraint. Let us examine in more detail the case that can be advanced in support of these views.

36

RESTRICTING UNION PROTECTION IN AN INDUSTRIAL DISPUTE

One of the main aims of the Act is to narrow the protection which the 1906 Act gave to trade unions and their funds outside the area of direct contractual liability. One effect of this is to add considerably to the number of situations in which trade union officials or trade union representatives may find themselves outside the law. For our purposes the point to note is that scattered throughout the Act there are a number of different industrial situations where action by groups of workers could result in union officials or union representatives coming before the National Industrial Relations Court, for allegedly committing an 'unfair industrial practice'. The most important of these situations include actions:

1 to bring about the breach of a legally enforceable collective agreement;
2 against non-unionists *qua* non-unionists;
3 to enforce unfair dismissal as defined in the Act;
4 to interfere with an application for an agency shop or approved closed shop;
5 to interfere with a compulsory ballot or cooling off period under the provisions of the Act;
6 to obtain union recognition when a case on this issue is lodged with the CIR;
7 to obtain union recognition when a recommendation on this issue goes against a given union at the CIR;
8 to prevent the cancellation of existing union recognition against the recommendations of the CIR;
9 bringing about the breach of the contract of an 'extraneous party' to a given industrial dispute;
10 bringing about the breach of an employment contract or commercial contract;
11 'in support' of any action listed under 1–10 above.

In line with traditionalist ideas of focusing on measures designed to foster union restraint on their members in general, the Act, in various different specific forms, produces the result

37

that actions of this kind give rise to union liability if the union or its agents have either 'knowingly induced' them or threatened to do so. This presents union leaders with a range of problems. First, given the list above, it is extremely likely that in most unions acts of this sort take place from time to time – often as a result of spontaneous shop-floor responses to perceived problems. (e.g. action against non-unionists, or minorities who refuse to come out on strike, or action against those who foment opposition to group policy or join breakaway organisations.) Similarly affected would seem to be action against an employer without due notice, or in breach of procedure, or action that prevents him from discharging his commercial obligations, or which interferes with the business of a third party.

Here it must be noted that in the past most acts of this kind have either been lawful or unlawful only in respect of individuals. But this is not the only new feature of the situation. In the past, although there were parts of the 1906 Act which were still a matter of controversy, unions could find out roughly what its most important sections meant. It is accepted that in the case of any new Act this is not possible, especially where it lists a whole range of new unlawful practices as this one does. As a result nobody can say precisely where the legal boundaries of strike action lie at the present time. It is impossible to tell who is likely to be counted as 'an extraneous party' or what action will be thought to be 'in support' of any of the acts listed under the other ten headings above. Most important of all, as has already been seen in the cases involving the Transport and General Workers' Union, words like 'inducement' are capable of different interpretations and different courts can give different answers to the question: Just what does a union have to do to demonstrate that it is not authorising a given unfair industrial practice?

To judge from a recent decision in the Lords, part of the answer lies in something termed 'implied authority' which depends on the custom and practice of the union and the habits of the individual work group. Much depends, it seems, on the wording of different union rule-books, and it could be that individual shop steward handbooks are also relevant. It is important to realise that problems of this kind in no way affect the argument that the Act may have important restraining effects; on the contrary in the words of *Fair Deal at Work* all these provisions may be said to strengthen 'the hands of employers, trade unions and individuals who resist irresponsible, subversive or unconstitutional action'.[4] And this is so, not merely because they continue to make all kinds of unofficial and unconstitutional action unlawful *per se*, but also because the penumbra of uncertainty which they create around the lawful limits of official and constitutional action should have the effect of creating doubts in the minds of trade union leaders about how far they are wise to urge militant attitudes upon their members in general. As a consequence, traditionalists may fairly hope that a premium will be placed on avoiding industrial action wherever possible – so that union officials may be induced to spend much of their time counselling moderation and looking for a way of disciplining those who refuse to accept their advice.

Of course, it may be said that the traditionalist functions of the Act are weakened by the fact that unions can always escape part of their impact by deciding to register, but it is important not to exaggerate the advantages that accrue from registration. It is true that one of the most important of the forms of liability which are included in the Act – an action for inducing a breach of an employment or commercial contract – does not apply where the union involved is registered and prepared to authorise what is done (e.g. action in respect of item 9 above). If liabilities are incurred under any of the other nine headings listed compensation is limited in the case of any one unlawful practice in respect of registered unions.

But too much should not be made of these two points. First, it has been argued that some of the actions brought against unregistered unions under item 10 above – i.e. those involving a breach of commercial contracts – might in the case of a registered union be actionable under item 9, on the grounds that they also involved unlawful action against an 'extraneous party'. Second, the limitation on compensation is not as far-reaching as might be thought. It applies to anyone proceeding against a union for alleged unfair practices. A series of proceedings arising out of a single industrial dispute can each result in the need to pay additional compensation; thus total damages may be extremely high, even for a registered union. (Indeed the provisions of item 11 listed above may be said to make this quite likely.) Finally, the limitation on financial liabilities for registered unions does not extend to costs. Normally a union that fails to establish the legality of its acts before the Court will be expected to pay the costs of both sides, and these have often been the most expensive item involved.

On balance then it can be said that these parts of the Act seem on the face of it to be well designed to carry forward the traditionalist attack on union rights and privileges in the interests of bargaining restraint and responsibility. What can be said about their reformist functions?

The most obvious way in which supporters of the Act try to establish a link between restrictions on union freedom in relation to strike liability and the reforms of collective bargaining along Donovan lines is by arguing that the former helps to bring about a 'restructuring' of the strike weapon that is essential if we are to move in the Donovan direction. Reference is made to what Donovan said about the rising rate of unofficial and unconstitutional strikes in many industries and firms. These were said to be harmful, largely because they were unpredictable and unanticipated and because, partly for this reason, they often had widespread and damaging secondary effects in other industries. This 'psychological cost' of unofficial and unconstitutional strikes was indeed stressed by the Commission itself. They argued that it was the fear of strikes of this sort that often discouraged firms from introducing new techniques and processes, and which produced desires for what may be termed a 'quiet life' amongst British managers.

By contrast, it is suggested, Britain would benefit from a move towards a different kind of strike activity – namely official strikes which take place at predictable points in the bargaining process, especially at the end of fixed-term agreements when a whole range of issues could be considered and dealt with together. Naturally, it is said, strikes of this kind might be expected to be larger and somewhat longer than old-style strikes, but they would also be more predictable and cause less trouble to a firm's customers or suppliers.

This suggestion in the past has often been linked in the minds of traditionalists with arguments in favour of a more American system of industrial relations – for it is undeniable that in the United States this kind of strike is far more common than in Britain. In *Fair Deal at Work*, for example, it is claimed that American disputes are much less damaging in economic and psychological terms than British disputes, precisely because they are predictable and occur at the end of fixed-term contracts. Mr Gunter's comments as Minister of Labour in 1967 are used to illustrate this point:

> When Mr. Walter Reuther brings his men out on strike in the American motor car industry, they have had at least three years' peace. No one has broken a contract. When he takes them back, there is another three years in which they can plan and wait. The dilemma of British industry is continuous interruption of production lines. No one knows when it will strike next.[5]

By imposing legal sanctions on all those who induce unconstitutional and unofficial strikes, it is argued, the Act should help to promote a most desirable shift in this direction – i.e. towards a more 'structured' and Americanised use of the strike weapon by British unions.

It is easy to see how all this can be made to seem particularly relevant to moves in the direction of Donovan-style plant and company agreements, if only because they too would seem to require a more controlled and structured use of the strike weapon. It is also possible to argue, as the Act's supporters have, that this kind of development ought to promote another American practice – the distinction between so-called 'disputes of right' and 'disputes of interest'. By the former is meant disputes over the interpretation and application of a given agreement that arise during the period of its operation. By the latter is meant disagreements over the re-negotiation of such an agreement, at a time when it is due for renewal. American unions usually accept that 'disputes of right' ought not to be settled by the use of industrial action of any kind. They are prepared to accept mediation, leading if necessary to a form of mutually binding arbitration as a final means of settlement. Strikes and other forms of industrial action are supposed to be kept in reserve, for use in 'disputes of interest' which only tend to arise when a collective contract is up for renewal.

Support for ideas of this kind, and their compatibility with Donovan-style plant and company agreements, are to be found in the government's recommended *Industrial Relations Code of Practice*. Indeed, it is in this document that the Department of Employment stresses the compatibility of rule enforcement and rule reform in the most developed way to date: it is suggested that freedom from the disruptive and time-wasting effects of unofficial and unconstitutional strikes should mean that both sides have more time to concentrate on long-term bargaining reform. Moreover, experiment and initiative should be easier to encourage in the new relaxed environment.

THE PROMOTION OF LEGALLY ENFORCEABLE AGREEMENTS

Prior to the publication of the Industrial Relations Bill the proposal that collective agreements in this country should be made legally enforceable was, perhaps, the most widely discussed recommendation of the traditionalist critique. Yet for the most part traditionalists seldom said precisely what they meant by this, and in this connection *Fair Deal at Work* was no exception. For the most part the view was taken that the great barrier to legal enforceability was contained in Section 4(4) of the 1871 Trade Union Act. This, in fact, only prevented the 'direct' enforcement of collective agreements between trade unions and employers' associations – and largely as the result of a legal quirk that defined employers' associations as trade unions. Agreements between unions and individual employers were not affected by the 1871 Act, they could always be directly enforced if those who signed them wished this to be the case. Much more important was the fact that the parties to collective agreements in this country have, by and large, not wanted to create legal

42

relationships. Moreover the agreements they have signed have rarely taken a legal form, and in many cases would have been regarded by the courts as 'void for uncertainty'.

Donovan took the view that the statutory limitations that might be said to be preventing the growth of legally enforceable agreements ought to be removed – for this reason they proposed the repeal of Section 4(4) of the 1871 Act. But they were opposed to hasty action designed to give legal status to the mass of existing collective agreements – especially the defective and inappropriate framework of industry-wide disputes procedures, which they thought should be scrapped as soon as possible.

One may assume that it is partly because the authors of the Act were convinced by at least some of the Donovan arguments that they framed their proposals in the way they did. To begin with, they agreed to leave existing agreements as they were – apart from abolishing section 4(4) of the 1871 Act. Secondly, although they did recommend a change in the status of *new* agreements designed to promote legal enforceability, they were content to do this in an indirect way which did not involve immediate compulsion. In effect the Act provides that written agreements signed after its implementation will be presumed by the Courts to constitute a legal contract between unions and employers unless they contain a clause stating 'that the agreement or part of it is intended not to be legally enforceable' (Section 34). This means that if unions can persuade employers to insert such a clause, their agreements need have no legal status. If employers will not agree to a so-called 'exclusion clause' of this kind unions can either refuse to sign *any* agreement, or sign without an exclusion clause something which immediately becomes a legal document.

It is also important to notice that if trade unions fail to obtain an exclusion clause, Section 36 of the Act creates additional obligations for them. It stipulates that the signatories of a legally enforceable agreement have to do more than observe it themselves. They must 'take all such steps as are reasonably practicable' to prevent persons from acting or purporting to act on their behalf from taking any action in breach of collective agreement. In the case of trade unions this means 'preventing members of the organisation from taking any such action'. Failure to do so makes them liable for an action for breach of contract, which could result in an award of extensive compensation. There is also the related point mentioned earlier that to induce anyone to break a legally enforceable collective agreement is itself an unfair industrial practice.

Finally, there are provisions in the Act to impose a legally enforceable procedure at the level of a plant or company in certain circumstances. Where existing agreements are thought to be defective, non-existent, or frequently contravened, application may be made by an employer, the government or a registered union to the National Industrial Relations Court. There is then an investigation by the CIR, who may draw up proposals for a legally enforceable procedure to fit the given circumstances. Action by one of the parties through the NIRC may then result in an order imposing the new agreement as a legally enforceable contract on the other (Section 40).

The relationship between these proposals and traditionalist thinking is obvious. It is rooted in the frequently expressed traditionalist belief restated in *Fair Deal at Work* that 'the fact that Britain is the only industrial country where agreements between employers and unions are not legally binding'[6] is crucial to an understanding of the British strike pattern. It follows that if we can promote a situation where more agreements are binding, and establish union responsibility to 'use their best endeavours' to secure their observance, we are likely to reduce the incidence of unofficial and unconstitutional strikes. In such a situation, it is argued, British unions, like American unions and those in other countries, would be forced to impose discipline on those members who threatened to expose the union to an action for breach of contract. As the Inns of Court Conservative and Unionist Society put the point in their evidence to the Donovan Commission:

If ... the employer has rights against a trade union to enforce collective agreements and the union itself has rights against its members who broke such an agreement, this would greatly strengthen responsible union leadership and would equally we think be a powerful basis for securing the observance of collective agreements.[7]

So much for the traditionalist roots of these parts of the Act; what of their compatibility with reformist ideas? On the reform side, it has been argued that provisions of this sort can only help forward the Donovan Commission's proposals for a more formal and comprehensive network of plant and company agreements, given the rather novel way in which they have been drafted in this Act. This is said to be because the existence or threat of legal obligations will make the parties more careful about the agreements they sign. They will avoid vague phrases and uncertainties of the kind that abound in British agreements; they may even look to lawyers to provide them with clear and precise phraseology in a way that will help to promote Donovan's more 'ordered' and 'stable' system still further. Above all, because the consequences of falling out and breaking agreements in the future will be so serious and expensive, both sides will be concerned to express their intentions to each other in clear, comprehensive and formal terms. As Sir Geoffrey Howe has put it in the very phraseology of the Donovan Commission:

> We believe that these provisions of the Act will therefore encourage both employers and unions to frame more precise and comprehensive agreements, as well as to consider more carefully what it is they are committing themselves to and how these commitments can be made effective.[8]

It may also be argued that the spread of legal enforceability will tend to concentrate negotiations at plant and company level – if only because as Donovan suggested these are the levels where the parties will find it easiest to spell out what needs to be done in ways that can be rigidly observed. Again these ideas are given support in the *Industrial Relations Code of Practice*, which recommends more formalisation, and concentration on agreements that can be 'effectively applied at the place of work'.[9] Underlying this prognosis there is the assumption that the legal environment created by the Act will provide a more suitable setting for a whole series of industrial relations reforms.

UNION SECURITY AND THE REFORM OF BARGAINING STRUCTURE

Many of the provisions of the Act are clearly designed to implement a major theme of the traditional view; the creation of a body of legislation which will, in the language of *Fair Deal at Work*, provide new safeguards for the individual against the exercise of 'excessive, unfair or harmful authority' by trade unions. To this end the Act's 'guiding principles' are intended to 'ensure that the membership can exercise reasonable democratic control in union government'.[10] The Act also provides a registration procedure designed to ensure that registered unions at least have rules which are formed to include provisions to protect the individual against 'excesses' of trade union power. However, these aims also found favour with the Donovan Commission, which did not suggest that they were incompatible with either its reformist intentions or its support for strong and effective trade unionism. It is true that the Act goes somewhat further than the Commission in some of its proposals for supervising and controlling internal union relations, but the supporters of the Act could reasonably claim that this was only a matter of degree.

More crucially the Act also contains provisions which reflect opposition to the closed shop in all its forms, together with other sections designed partly to test the 'representativeness' of unions. These proposals are obviously justifiable in terms of traditionalist assumptions about the 'voluntary' nature of unions, and the need to prevent them being captured by 'subversives'. What must be considered, in this section, is the case for suggesting that these parts of the Act can also be squared with Donovan objectives.

In the case of the closed shop it is necessary to stress once again that this is not allowed in any form under the Act. It is unlawful to insist that the only alternative a worker has to joining and remaining a member of a union is leaving the job. In the case of the pre-entry shop, where membership is made a pre-condition of employment, the Act is quite unequivocal. Action to obtain a pre-entry shop is an unfair industrial practice and agreements designed to enforce it are to be regarded as void. What the Act does is to provide a partial alternative to the post-entry shop, where union membership is made a *subsequent* condition of employment. In fact two alternatives are provided, both confined to registered unions. They are the agency shop and the misleadingly titled 'approved closed shop'.

Essentially the difference between these two forms of 'union security agreement' is that one contains one more option than the other. Thus the worker in an agency shop can choose from one of *two* additional alternatives that are not available to the worker in the normal post-entry shop: either he can elect to pay an equivalent in union dues to the union but still decline to join; or he can, if he prefers, invoke a procedure which results in him paying the same amount of money to a nominated charity on the grounds that he is a 'conscientious objector'. In the so-called 'approved closed shop', which is difficult to obtain, only the second option is available. In neither case is it possible to have a conscientious objection to paying the money.

Presumably the case against the pre-entry closed shop, and the absence of any kind of alternative to it in the Act, is the traditionalist desire to deny trade unions a means of controlling, or restricting, the supply of labour to a job or trade. In other words the practice is offensive mainly on economic grounds – it represents an abuse of union power which acts as a handicap on industrial efficiency. This is strictly in conformity with proposals in *Fair Deal at Work* and is rooted in its predecessor *A Giant's Strength*. The contrast with Donovan is clear, it drew attention to the fact that many groups of workers would be unable to develop and sustain effective bargaining without the entry control functions of the pre-entry closed shop.

However, it has been argued that by providing the agency shop as an alternative to the post-entry closed shop the Act goes a long way to recognising Donovan's arguments in favour of union security. The agency shop may also be justified on the grounds that it furthers Donovan's objectives of preventing multi-unionism within a particular grade of work as the closed shop itself undoubtedly does. Thus the Act 'recognises that in practice there are many real advantages for everyone in having unions which represent the whole of a particular group of

47

employees'.[11] It may also be argued that the agency shop represents a recognition by traditionalists of what has been termed the 'common obligation argument'. This argument, commonly used to justify the closed shop, suggests that those who benefit from union membership ought to be prepared to pay for the privilege – as American unionists put it, what is contested is the right of the non-unionist to be a 'free-rider' on the backs of the union majority. In the agency shop, unless one can gain acceptance as a conscientious objector, one is forced to pay one's share to the union that negotiates improvements in wages and conditions.

But the full extent of the argument that these parts of the Act are basically compatible with the Donovan Commission's views on these questions can only be assessed after mention is made of what we shall term its 'revocation procedures'. These are intimately related with those parts of the Act that deal with the reform of bargaining structure, another Donovan objective.

In contrast to the Commission, the Act links together three related aims:

1 The provision of legal support for trade unions seeking to obtain recognition from reluctant employers.
2 The reform of bargaining units and the elimination of multi-unionism.
3 Revocation procedures designed to test the 'representativeness' of unions which are already recognised by employers.

The central link between all three aims is the concept of the 'sole bargaining agency'. An application may be made for the recognition of one or more unions as a 'sole bargaining agent' to the NIRC. Applications will be considered from three sources: registered unions, employers, and the Secretary of State for Employment. The NIRC may decide to refer an application to the CIR, which then investigates the issues involved, and may or may not recommend the recognition of one or more unions as sole bargaining agent for a specified group of employees, termed a 'bargaining unit'. A strong set of unfair industrial practices operate against those who try to affect the issue in advance of, or contrary to, a CIR report.

If an employer continues to resist a report recommending a sole bargaining agent, those unions designated which are registered may apply for a CIR ballot of members of the bargaining unit. If a majority of those voting favour the recommendation, the NIRC can make an order directing recognition. (Non-compliance with such an order gives the unions concerned the right of unilateral and legally binding arbitration by the Industrial Arbitration Board.)

But the NIRC will also entertain an application for the withdrawal of a sole bargaining agency. If the agency arises as a result of a past NIRC order, two-fifths of the workers in the bargaining unit must signify their agreement in writing to such a course of action. If the union holding the bargaining agency has obtained it without the use of the Act, or before the passage of the Act, one-fifth of those affected must signify. In either case the CIR is asked to investigate, and once again a range of unfair industrial practices operate against those who attempt to set the decision aside. A similar revocation procedure can be invoked against an agreed or statutorily imposed agency shop on the grounds that the union concerned no longer has the support of the workers. A fifth of the workers affected must sign an application, and unless either two-thirds of those voting, or a majority of those eligible to vote, favour its continuance, the agency shop becomes unlawful.

Obviously the supporters of the Act can claim that this complex procedure is an advance on Donovan, though designed to promote similar objectives. To the claims of unions for recognition may be added the grievances of employers suffering from multi-unionism. Either side can start the procedure, the unions to force recognition on a reluctant employer, the employer to compel unions who are competing for members to get together to sort things out between them. In this way employers who have long had to recognise and bargain with several unions for the same group of workers could invoke the aid of the Act – for example, British Leyland, whose problems in this regard were recognised by the Commission. They would ask the CIR to tell them which union, or unions, they ought to stop recognising. Legal pressures could be deployed against any union that refused to accept the implications of a report of the CIR on matters of this kind.

At the same time the workers themselves are given their own procedure, which dovetails into that of the unions and employers. They can challenge the representativeness of any union, and seek to change the union that has the 'sole bargaining agency' for their bargaining unit. They can also challenge any union's right to an agency shop, if it fails to satisfy them. But in both cases they are unable to get far unless they can show that a significant number of the workers affected want a change, and there is always the CIR to which the union can appeal. Surely, if a case can be established in situations of this kind, say the Act's supporters, the workers will probably have already given their support to another more representative union. The way is then open for that union to apply for its own bargaining agency and agency shop. In this way the Act is securing a return to the stable situation the Donovan Commission wished to maintain.

In summary, what the Act's supporters are really suggesting throughout the case set out above is that (if one is careful enough and takes enough trouble to get the small print right) there is no essential conflict between restraint and reform. They can be combined together, if the mixture is sufficiently judicious; providing ways of moderating the undue powers and privileges of the unions, while at the same time advancing the cause of more formal plant and company comprehensive agreements. Indeed, in so far as one encourages a shift in the character of strikes, or a more careful and precise attitude towards negotiations, these aims are mutually reinforcing. The same is true of the traditionalist aims of protecting the individual worker against trade union abuse of power. Of course one has to do this in a way that assists, rather than frustrates, the simplification of bargaining units and the preservation of stability. But these things are difficult, rather than impossible. Everyone wants the best of both worlds: it is claimed the Act demonstrates that this desirable objective can be achieved in practice.

Notes

1 Speech to the Third Annual Forum of the Institute of Collective Bargaining and Group Relations, in New York.
2 Speech to the Industrial Law Society.
3 Donovan Report, Research Paper 10: *Shop Stewards and Workplace Relations*, by W. E. J. McCarthy and S. R. Parker, HMSO, 1968. See also, J. F. B. Goodman and T. G. Whittingham, *Shop Stewards in British Industry*, McGraw-Hill, 1969.
4 *Fair Deal at Work*, p. 29.
5 *Fair Deal at Work*, p. 28.
6 *Fair Deal at Work*, p. 31.
7 *Trade Unions for Tomorrow*, Conservative Political Centre, 1966, p. 35.
8 Speech to the Financial Times Conference on Industrial Relations, London, 28 October 1971.
9 Department of Employment, *Industrial Relations Code of Practice*, HMSO, 1972.
10 *Fair Deal at Work*, p. 20.
11 *Fair Deal Takes Shape*, Conservative Central Office, 1970, p. 16.

4. The case against the Act

'The case of the Five Dockers has jolted us out of the comfortable assumption that reform is achieved simply by passing an Act of Parliament pleasing to 51% or more of the nation and then handing it over to the courts to enforce with the aid of incantations about the rule of law.'

'There is no magic in a majority. To the other 49% its acts may appear as tyrannical as those of an autocrat. Surely Ulster today is showing us the consequences of the doctrine that a majority is always right and that a minority must always submit.'

LORD DEVLIN[1]

The approach in this chapter will be similarly concentrated on the three related sets of provisions that have been discussed in the previous chapter in developing the case for the Act; i.e. the restriction of union protection in an industrial dispute, the promotion of legally enforceable agreements and those relating to union security and the reform of bargaining structures.

Although we propose to comment on each aspect separately, it should be emphasised that the main lines of criticism we present below have a general relevance and do not only apply to the parts of the Act we have discussed so far. It is an essential part of our case that the Act is for the most part based on mistaken assumptions concerning the nature of trade union leadership. Because these assumptions have had a crucial influence on the Act in its entirety, our criticisms are intended to have a wider relevance, extending far beyond that part of the Act around which they happen to be formulated in the discussion that follows.

RESTRICTING UNION PROTECTION IN AN
INDUSTRIAL DISPUTE

The crucial weakness of the Act's provisions in this field is the assumption that the creation of an ambit of fear and uncertainty around the extent of union liability for strike action, will transform union leadership into an instrument for bargaining restraint. The Act creates a situation where union leaders are made uneasily aware that at any time their members may be laying the union open to an action for compensation unless they prevent them from behaving as they normally do. The framers of the Act have not thought through the likely consequences of this situation. It is not designed to create the strong and stable trade unionism that Donovan saw as an essential prerequisite of effective plant and company bargaining. It will not help union leaders to establish the degree of trust and receptivity to official advice that must be created if a more formal and predictable system of industrial relations is to develop in this country.

This is largely because the Act presents union officials with a series of intolerable choices whenever it is activated against them in the context of an industrial dispute. To illustrate their nature we will discuss a series of alternative strategies which a local union official might adopt if a section of his members appears to be taking a course of action that may involve the union in an unfair industrial practice – such as discrimination against non-unionists, a form of illegal picketing, a strike without due notice, action involving a breach of some other type of contract, or action in defiance of a ruling of one or another of the institutions of the Act. Four options are open to the official at this point.

In the first place he may decide to use all his influence and authority to prevent the contemplated action, and if it takes place he may ask the relevant body in the union to authorise appropriate disciplinary action. (And, as we have said, following the House of Lords judgement in the case of *Midland Cold Storage* v. *Transport and General Workers' Union* this would probably involve, at the very least, withdrawing the credentials of

c

any shop stewards involved.) A number of hazardous possibilities open up for the union official who decides to take this line. In the first place the members may ignore his advice, the employer or workers involved may sue, and the stewards may turn out to have acted lawfully after all. (More accurately, it may not be possible for the plaintiff to prove that they have acted unlawfully.) In this case the official will look rather foolish, and will rapidly gain a reputation for unnecessary panic in the face of the enemy. His reputation will not be improved even when he is generally thought to be right on the law, if it transpires that the stewards were right when they said 'this company will never go to law'.

But let us suppose that the official is right, and an action is brought which ends in an injunction ordering a return to work. The official is still in a difficult position. Traditionalists always assume that workers who are told that their proposed method of prosecuting a grievance is against the law will abandon it forthwith. Recent events hardly bear out this view. What is the union official to do if things develop differently? Traditionalists will reply of course that a change will come over the labour force once the official threatens them with disciplinary action in the name of the union. Of course this may happen, but then again it may not.

What is much more likely is that action on the part of the union to uphold or reinforce a court decision will divide the members into two conflicting groups; those who think the union has no alternative and those who consider that it has 'sold the pass'. Again the traditionalists may say 'So much the worse for the union, if it cannot command the support of its members it deserves to have disunity.' But this is hardly the point.

The fact is that in many instances a simple injunction to obey the law so that the union funds can be protected is likely to create a divisive and disruptive situation within any union, and union officials are paid to take this into account. Moreover, action of this sort is likely to be still more destructive of rank and file loyalty if the union official appears to be receiving his orders from above – say from a far away and little known authority like the average union national executive, or general secretary. And the more the dispute is in an advanced stage, so that tempers have risen and positions have been adopted, the more difficult it will be to avoid poisoning the atmosphere. All this is not to deny that sometimes, when the union points out that their actions are unlawful, union members will be influenced. But here a great deal will depend on the attitude of the shop steward. The trouble with the Act is that it does not allow the official to leave it to the steward.

As the Donovan research showed, stewards tend to be a moderating influence on the shop floor.[2] But as they also pointed out, stewards are essentially 'consensual' in their leadership style. That is to say they have to persuade their members to follow their preferred course of action. They have no way of compelling anyone – until and unless the majority decide to adopt the steward's viewpoint as their own. Of course, stewards who can usually persuade their members are usually trusted when there is no time to explain, but in the long run all stewards work by their ability to convince 'the meeting' that they are right. And the custom of the shop floor is that if they fail in this they must accept their side of the bargain – i.e. they are expected to adopt and fight for the majority view as if it were their own. This is why stewards who lose a vote usually go out of their way to stress that they fully accept and will seek to loyally advance the collective decision.

Full-time officials are well aware of all this, but it does not help them in dealing with the Act. They know that if they are to influence the membership they must carry the stewards with them. But the stewards know that if they are to remain the trusted leaders of the shop floor they must ultimately abide by the decisions of the work-group – even if this involves disagreeing with the union. Sensible officials are normally quite prepared to accept this, as the price of continued steward influence and the chance to use them to persuade the shop floor to take union advice in future. But the Act makes this kind of tolerance impossible if the union wishes to avoid financial responsibility for the consequences of the essential conditions of shop-floor leadership. And it is important to realise that the problem for the union official does not stop when the union agrees to discipline the steward, by withdrawing his credentials. For in this instance it purchases its own financial immunity at the cost of laying the steward open to an action for inducing an unfair industrial practice 'in his personal capacity'. It has been said, with some justification, that this may turn out to be a recipe for a new generation of trade union martyrs, as seemed to be the case recently in the docks when action was taken against shop stewards as individuals and they were eventually imprisoned. What it will not do is help to bring about the closer relationship between unions and the members that Donovan wanted to encourage. What then of the other alternatives open to our local official?

They are more easily dealt with, but no more viable in the end. The simplest reaction would be to decide that the Act was much too complicated to try to understand, and that in the circumstances the less one seeks to know about whether it is likely to be breached or not, the better. In fact some overworked and less responsible full-time officials are already adopting this view. They have made it clear that they wish to know as little as possible about what is going on among their membership, and the Act encourages them in this view. Requests for guidance about its meaning and implications are answered evasively, or by reference to head office. It is true that stewards are not antagonised by precipitate or over-zealous concern for union funds, but they are also not helped when they look like getting into trouble. A moment's reflection reveals that this is not really a tenable position and the more trouble that arises the less tenable it becomes. In any case it is hardly the kind of union leadership that the sponsors of the Act or the members of the Donovan Commission would wish to see encouraged.

A more sophisticated reaction, which already has its devotees, might be termed the position of qualified and reluctant hypocrisy. In effect the official seeks to take the stewards and their members into his confidence, to get them to accept the need for him to appear to observe the legal niceties of the Act. Thus members are told that the official must never be asked to support a strike to obtain or maintain the closed shop, although he is known to be tacitly in favour of various kinds of pressure on non-unionists. Officially he must always require the members to give due notice of strike action, although he will always be prepared to negotiate a return to work on more favourable terms if they ignore his advice. When 'secondary boycott' action of doubtful legality is planned the official advises his stewards how to avoid laying themselves open to actions for 'inducement' by limiting their own formal involvement to that of passing on information. In exchange they are asked to accept that if things go wrong he will have to publicly 'recommend' a return to normal working and disown their action.

The attractions of this approach for the subtle and resourceful official should be obvious, but it can involve a great deal of time and effort and may easily go wrong. Senior stewards may understand the complexity and deviousness that has been forced upon their union official, but to those not in his confidence such behaviour may sometimes appear to be unnecessarily inconsistent and even dishonest. There is also the problem that confidences are not always kept, and can be unintentionally broken. Moreover some of the best union officials, who think that honest and straightforward dealing are an essential part of the image of the successful and influential bargainer, do not easily take to this kind of behaviour pattern. But of course the main reason why the policy of qualified hypocrisy is not really viable is that it fails to deal with the nub of the problem posed above. It cannot prevent the situation arising where a union is faced with the critical choice – withdraw the steward's credentials or pay the financial penalty. And it provides no way of dealing with this problem when it does arise.

The final option open to our full-time official is defiance of the law. He tries to suggest to members ways of advancing their objectives that do not lay the union open to legal action. Where this is not possible he preaches restraint. But if his advice is ignored and an action is sustained he does not favour disowning the stewards in order to protect union funds. He argues that either the union must pay itself, or suffer the procedure of 'sequestration' under the Act. (This procedure enables the Court to seize the union assets long enough to pay itself the money.)

57

Of course many left-wing trade unionists have already argued that this is the only honest and decent action to adopt given the iniquities of the Industrial Relations Act. Fortunately we do not have to consider the justifiability or reasonableness of this argument at the moment. Our point is simply that this course does not avoid the dilemma posed above – it settles it permanently one way, and it could be very expensive. After all, decisions of this magnitude cannot be left to individual union officials or their local committees. They involve decisions at national level, and action of this kind would probably need to be upheld by the union's supreme decision-taking body – e.g. its annual conference. What a union decides to do at this level for one group it can hardly deny to others. Once openly committed to a policy of this sort even the most wealthy of unions could eventually find itself in severe financial trouble.

Naturally the hard-line traditionalist may refuse to see the problem. These transitional difficulties, he may say, are inevitable if we are to force British unions to accept their responsibilities. The threat of bankruptcy, in this situation, simply helps to concentrate the mind. All one can say is that this is a point of view. But it is not that of the Donovan Commission. They went out of their way to stress the consensual nature of union leadership at all levels. Their proposals assume that a union leader's influence, which is needed to gain shop-floor acceptance for their more structured and ordered system of agreements, does not derive from his office, or ability to invoke the rule-book; it is rooted in the membership's awareness of his responsiveness to their demands and wishes. This is seen most clearly at the level of the steward, but at any level the union official who abdicates this aspect of his role can hardly claim the title of leader – especially in the present climate where authority structures are being increasingly questioned both on the shop floor and in the rest of society.

If union leadership is of this nature it cannot be developed and assisted by placing it in a position where it may often have to tell the rank and file that whatever they may decide the leader's course of action is pre-ordained, fixed by an external legal authority. This will be particularly unacceptable, of course, where members are taking action that is customary, and is seen to be necessary to secure an effective redress of their grievances. It was because they realised this that the Donovan Commission said repeatedly that traditionalist solutions which involved leaning on union officials did not get 'to the root of the problem'. No amount of careful drafting can alter this fact.

On examination, then, the argument that making unions liable for the unlawful acts of their stewards in an industrial dispute will help bargaining reform is based on the unlikely assumption that it will work – in the sense that most unofficial and unconstitutional strikes can be prevented in this way, thus clearing the way for the peaceful transformation of the British industrial relations. But this is to assume precisely what needs to be proved; namely that union leaders possess a reserve fund of power or influence over their members which they can be frightened into using by the threat of union bankruptcy. This must in turn be based on one of two even more unlikely assumptions; either the leaders themselves foment most strikes or the members blunder into them in an absent-minded way, rather than using the proper procedures.

Of course there may still be a few hard-line traditionalists who believe all this. The rest of us may beg leave to doubt it, and when we do it is not difficult to imagine a more credible picture: A growth of disorder and unfocused militancy, alongside a harassed and weakened trade union leadership. Full-time union officials who are less willing than they were to offer honest and straightforward advice, including, if need be, counsels of caution and moderation. Shop stewards torn between the threat of personal legal liability, if their union manages to disown them, and the need to honour the decisions of their members. It is difficult to see how all this would help the proposals of the Donovan Commission, or produce a more informed and rational discussion of industrial relations problems on the shop floor. It is much more likely to lead to a shortage of shop stewards – for only a fool, or a genuine revolutionary, is likely to want the job on these terms.

THE PROMOTION OF LEGALLY ENFORCEABLE
COLLECTIVE AGREEMENTS

Given the argument developed above it should be obvious why
the Act's provisions to encourage the spread of legally enforceable procedures are also unlikely to work as intended. Once
again the trade union leader who is unfortunate enough to
operate within the legal restrictions created by them may find
that unreal and impractical policy-making functions are foisted
upon him. Indeed the Act insists that unless unions can obtain
employer agreement to an exclusion clause they have to do
more than merely cut themselves off from their stewards if
unlawful action is proved. The additional obligation is then
placed on them to 'take all such steps as are reasonably practicable' to prevent and if necessary bring to an end any breach
of the agreement by their members.

At the time of writing, so far as we are aware, no case involving a legally enforceable agreement has been brought before the
Courts. Consequently the precise meaning and extent of this
phrase is more than usually delphic. Presumably some courts,
in some instances, could argue that union funds were liable
unless all the workers involved had been threatened with
expulsion. (Some might even expect such threats to be carried
out before a given union could avoid liability.) Once again this
sort of presumption is compatible with the *agent provocateur* view
of union leadership, or with the assumption that union members
can be easily dissuaded from action in breach of the law once
the consequences are pointed out to them. Those who operate
with a more complex model of the industrial relations system
will again beg leave to doubt the possibility of combining
measures of this sort with the aim of stable and effective trade
unionism.

But there are also a number of special features about the way
this Act seeks to encourage legal enforceability which need to
be stressed at this stage. The first point to note is that the Act
adopts an unusually wide definition of what may count as an
enforceable agreement in the future. As the *TUC Handbook* on
the Act says, the presumption of enforceability, in the absence
of a specific exclusion clause, applies:

. . . to any written settlement governing terms and conditions of employment or industrial relations procedure or both. It will apply whether the settlement is at national, district or local level. It will apply to the written decisions of national joint industrial councils, local works councils, shop floor negotiating committees and all intermediate joint negotiating committees alike.[3]

Moreover, it is not possible, it seems, to cover the meetings and decisions of bodies of this kind by signing a *general* exclusion clause. As the TUC puts it, 'every decision, award or minute of a joint negotiating body must contain an exclusion clause if it is not to be regarded as legally enforceable'.[4] Not unnaturally they conclude: 'This could be effected by means of a rubber stamp.'[5]

As is well known, most unions have been able to persuade most employers to operate what may be termed the 'rubber stamp' procedure, at least in the case of industry-wide agreements and formal plant and company agreements where full-time union officials are involved. Indeed reports indicate that most personnel managers and experienced line managers are only too willing to comply with this request. They have their own rubber stamp and are eager to deploy it, if only to reassure the unions they deal with that they have no desire to foist upon them the ambiguous and potentially disruptive effects of the 'reasonably practicable' clause. On the other hand, one may doubt how far the average shop steward and first line supervisor always remembers to wield the rubber stamp at all times in works committee meetings, placing it alongside each and every minute. There is thus the difficulty that they may be creating legal relationships without intending to, and it is reasonable to expect trade unions to be worried about this situation. There is also the danger that not all employers will be as scrupulously fair as the majority have been so far – i.e. they will fail to point out to their stewards the far-reaching requirements of the Act. Thus the potential threat to the union remains, and unions have to consider what steps are appropriate to reduce this threat to the minimum. Unfortunately for the aims of the Donovan

Commission and the claims of the supporters of the Act, the obvious course to adopt is to advise stewards that as far as possible they should, in future, sign no written agreements at all. In other words, the Act places a premium on informality on the shop floor, for what is not written down, in agreements, or minutes, or even in the form of written undertakings exchanged by letter after the settlement of a dispute, is much less likely to give rise to *post-hoc* legal obligations. As the TUC guide to the Act puts this point:

> . . . although oral agreements which are clear enough could conceivably be legally enforceable this is most unlikely. Unions may therefore wish to enter into an oral agreement rather than a written agreement which does not incorporate a clause excluding legal enforceability, but union representatives should ensure that there are witnesses to such agreements.[6]

Given the status accorded to legal agreements by the Act, and the general ambit of legal uncertainty it creates, it is difficult to criticise the TUC for giving such advice to member unions at the present time; but if it is followed to any substantial extent it will mean the end of Donovan-type bargaining reform. As has been stressed above, and as will be developed further in the next chapter, it is an essential element of the change that the Commission wished to see introduced in bargaining systems that there should be a major move away from reliance on 'oral agreements'. Most particularly, at the level of the shop floor, the aim is to create a situation where stewards naturally turn to formalisation as a way of dealing with their problems. The argument is that if workers and their representatives can be made to see the relevance and utility of more formal and precise jointly agreed rules, negotiated within the enterprise to fit its special circumstances, this is likely to do more to prevent the sudden and wayward use of industrial action than any general framework of external legal regulation. The tragedy now is that the form taken by this part of the Act may produce a major obstacle to this process. Moreover, this is all the more likely because of the imposition procedures of the Act mentioned earlier.

It will be remembered that they provide that where existing agreements are frequently contravened, either an employer or the Secretary of State for Employment may invoke Sections 37 or 45 of the Act and demand a reference to the CIR. The CIR may then draw up a legally enforceable procedure for application to the unions concerned – whether they are prepared to sign it or not. (One may doubt how far an imposed procedure of this kind ought to be called an agreement as such – at best it would appear to be what the French term a 'fictitious agreement' – but that is not the most important point at the moment.) The crucial fact is that in so far as the threat of the use of the imposition procedure becomes and remains a factor in negotiations on the union side it must surely act as a disincentive to formalisation and precision. For formalisation and precision, though it has real advantages for unions, almost invariably means accepting restrictions on their freedom to react in conventional ways.

Thus a new job evaluation scheme, while it extends the steward's right to participate in job assessment, also tends to restrict the kind of arguments he can use to obtain a wage increase for groups of his members. Similarly jointly agreed disciplinary codes, though they restrict managerial prerogatives, and extend new job rights to most workers, usually rule out certain grounds that were available in the past for objecting to dismissal. Most important of all, the new and tailor-made procedures that Donovan wanted to see invariably involve a mixture of new rights and obligations for shop stewards themselves. Under old-style agreements, rights of access to management were restricted, but capable of being supplemented by all kinds of understandings that were often useful to stewards. New agreements may give them more extended formal rights, but they may also be less easy to get round. More crucially, perhaps, under old-style agreements stewards were only expected to exhaust the procedure, or give due notice, before they became involved in strike action. Under new arrangements one hopes they will be persuaded to follow American patterns of behaviour – agreeing to give up the right to all strike action over specified issues for the duration of an agreement. (In this case they would

63

exchange the right to strike for access to binding arbitration, but once again this would involve new patterns of behaviour and restrictions on the type of arguments they could use to process members' grievances.)

The question is whether developments of this sort are to be assisted by vague threats about the use of the Act's imposition provisions. Of course supporters of the Act may reply that the government would not be foolish enough to invoke these provisions where unions were doing their best to negotiate and apply more precise and formal procedures. The problem is whether assurances of this kind are likely to be taken at their face value in the present climate. The danger is that the fear that they could be invoked, given the general background of legal uncertainty, may constitute yet another difficulty that has to be overcome by those on the union side who wish to continue to make the case for Donovan-type bargaining experiments.

The argument that a presumption in favour of legal enforcement helps to foster bargaining reform turns out to be no more tenable than the suggestion that this is helped by extending union liability in an industrial dispute. Both assume what needs to be proved – in this instance the readiness of unions to accept and even welcome a new and untried legal obligation to 'take all such steps as are reasonably practicable' to restrain their members.

The fact is that legal enforceability only makes sense on one of two diametrically opposed assumptions, and neither of these leads to the way in which it is 'encouraged' by the Act. The first is the hard-line traditionalist position, that new legal restrictions of all kinds must be fastened on unions regardless of the costs to bargaining reform. But those taking this view should, in logic, advocate an Act stipulating that at some time in the near future *all* existing and future agreements between unions and employers will be presumed to give rise to legal obligations, whatever the parties may say to the contrary. The framers of the Act drew back from this, partly because they accepted Donovan's criticisms concerning the adequacy of most existing agreements. But their reasonableness in this respect has not helped them to be consistent.

64

The only logical alternative to this view is that advocated by the Commission itself. The law should content itself with being neutral. Any restrictions on the ability of the parties to give rise to enforceable obligations ought to be removed – such as Section 4(4) of the 1871 Act. After that matters should be left to the parties; their intentions should be left to the courts to determine as and when required, without any 'presumptions' inserted by statute.

In chapter Eight this approach is developed further, and the view is taken that the free assumption of legal relationships, within a neutral legal framework, could be a desirable development symbolising a mutual commitment on the part of both unions and employers to move towards a different kind of bargaining style. But this would have to be a product of joint experience. It cannot be assisted by external legal products designed to fasten new and impractical duties on one side of the bargaining table.

UNION SECURITY AND THE REFORM OF BARGAINING STRUCTURES

The Act's supporters claim that it provides a way of reconciling the requirements of union security and the reform of bargaining structure with the need to protect workers as individuals from tyrannical union power and its abuses. Once again this is a claim that does not stand examination. The legitimate requirements of union security are not effectively protected. The provisions of the Act are more likely to encourage an increase in bargaining fragmentation. The most difficult problems of individual conscience and independence are not really dealt with and may be harder to solve as a result of the Act.

Let us begin with what the Act proposes to allow in place of the closed shop. Four major defects are to be found in these sections of the Act. First, there is no lawful substitute for the pre-entry shop. Workers, unlike professional men, such as doctors, solicitors, or members of the Inns of Court, are not to be allowed to practise lawful entry control. This may be justified on hard-line traditionalist grounds in respect of some well-organised craft groups, like newspaper workers (except that it is

65

unlikely that any law will have the slightest effect on what goes on in Fleet Street chapels). What cannot be justified on Donovan grounds is the refusal to allow groups like musicians, actors, or construction workers the right to lawfully operate any form of pre-entry shop. For most of these groups some control over the labour supply, in their extremely casual and shifting vocations, is an essential prerequisite of effective organisation. In their case the so-called 'approved closed shop' – i.e. the agency shop without one of its options – is a very poor second best. Second, the agency shop itself is only available to registered unions. The formal justification for this, of course, is that only registered unions have agreed to subject themselves to the internal disciplines of the Registrar. But in fact registration means very little to workers as individuals. As finally drafted the main drawbacks of registration, from the point of view of the union, arise out of the fact that it has to abide by the provisions of Schedule 4. But this Schedule is largely concerned with specifying the institutional provisions that union rule-books must cover, together with a list of administrative details. It may create many headaches for union officials but it is unlikely to have much impact on workers, at least as it stands at present.

Much more important are the standards of union behaviour set out in Part 4 of the Act, containing the so-called 'guiding principles'. For example, these principles do ensure that workers 'arbitrarily' or 'unreasonably' excluded from both registered and unregistered unions are given the right of legal redress and compensation. It is true that the unregistered trade union member has to use the Industrial Tribunals to get his legal rights under this part of the Act, whereas the registered trade unionist can also go to the Registrar. But these and other minor differences do not seem to us to justify withholding the right to the agency shop from non-registered unions.*

* The other substantial difference is that registered unions have to bring their rules into conformity with the 'guiding principles' *as a condition* of permanent registration. Unregistered unions can neglect to do so at the risk of members sustaining an action for unlawful expulsion. Once again this does not seem to us to be a difference justifying withholding all forms of union security arrangement from unregistered unions.

In fact one suspects that these parts of the Act have been unduly affected by the growing realisation on the part of its authors during its preparation that few TUC unions were likely to register. As a result it was important to find ways of regulating the internal behaviour of all kinds of organisations, while adding wherever possible to the advantages of registration as such. The drafters of the Act effected this compromise as best as they could, but this does not make the results logical or conducive to stable labour relations. In practice it has meant that over most of British industry today there is no lawful means of operating a substitute for the closed shop.

Third, there are the defects of the agency shop itself even where it is available. The best way to illustrate these is by reference to the organisational functions of its precursor, the post-entry closed shop. This device assisted trade union stability and effectiveness in two ways:

1 It helped to ensure that all workers in a given area were recruited and retained in the union.
2 It enabled the union to exercise additional disciplinary authority over the workers in that area.

The question is, how far does the agency shop provide an effective substitute for both these functions? In the case of the first the answer is to a limited extent. In the case of the second not at all.

As we have noted, workers cannot be made to belong to and remain members of a union with an agency shop; they can only be made to pay the equivalent in dues without joining, or a similar sum to a nominated charity of their choice. The authors of the Act may be right in assuming, somewhat cynically, that most people faced with the choice of having to pay the money will decide that they might as well join the union, but a lot may depend on how far the union is able to ensure that they do in fact pay regularly. Thus the man who opts to pay to a charity may not always continue to do so and it may be difficult for the union to ensure that he does. No doubt there will be disputes about this matter, with union members asserting that they 'know for a fact' that a group of would-be conscientious

67

objectors 'have not paid a penny to anybody for years'. In the end inquiries may be made to the charity concerned, but the whole procedure is likely to be cumbersome and a fertile ground for dispute and disagreement.

But this is not the only problem. The fact is that the agency shop has no disciplinary functions. Discipline is exerted in the closed shop because those who refuse to abide by union policies and decisions face the ultimate penalty of expulsion and exclusion from the job on grounds of non-unionism. This situation cannot arise in the agency shop. The most that can happen is that a person expelled for refusing to observe union policy can decide to pay the equivalent of dues to a nominated charity. A union who refuses to accept his right to do this is committing an unfair industrial practice.

The Donovan Commission found few signs that unions abused their powers in closed shop situations. By and large they were extremely reluctant to sanction expulsion from the union when exclusion from the job was involved. Nevertheless, this ultimate reserve power can be important, and it is paradoxical that those who complain so often that unions fail to exercise sufficient control over their members should want to weaken it. After all, the disciplinary functions of the closed shop can be of crucial importance in enabling moves to be made towards reformed bargaining structures, and in gaining support for more formal agreements. This kind of bargaining reform usually involves the introduction of more precise agreements and rules that inevitably involve certain restrictions on union freedom and flexibility. The workers in general must benefit on balance from these proposals, or the union could never gain their assent to them, but it is very often the case that there are more or less powerful minorities who have done well out of the existing system who wish to obstruct all forms of change. Thus when wage structures are reformed, those with very high piece-rates usually oppose reform of any kind. If new processes are required those who gained extremely high levels of overtime out of the old system frequently obstruct all talk of change.

The closed shop operates as an essential union security device in situations of this sort. If dissident minorities go too far in opposing worthwhile reforms that the majority want they can always be told, at the end of the day, that they have become union policy and must be accepted. If, as sometimes happens, they decide to 'tear up their cards' in protest the union knows that the ultimate sanction of the closed shop can be employed to ease them back into the union. The Donovan Commission accepted the validity of these arguments, together with the case advanced for the closed shop within a system of plant and company bargaining along American lines. In the United States, where there are stringent limitations on the use of strike action during the period of agreements, it is generally felt that formal and comprehensive closed shop agreements have played a crucial role in ensuring conformity to the rules. As the Commission put the point, in this situation 'the closed shop helps to secure the observance of agreements, since it adds to the power of the union to discipline those who ignore them.'[7]

But the overall impact of the Act on union security can only be assessed after examining the way in which the revocation procedures are likely to work in practice. (It will be remembered that they provide a means whereby minority groups can challenge existing bargaining arrangements and agency shop agreements.) There are a number of reasons for suggesting that these parts of the Act are likely to undermine union security still further and promote fractionalisation and sectionalism on the workers' side of the bargaining table.

To begin with the procedure provided positively encourages dissident action outside the confines of the union. Indeed, workers who have had no experience of a union working, since they have never been members at any time, can start the revocation procedures in train. (In fact a minority of non-members, in a given bargaining unit, could secure the disenfranchisement of a union that had satisfied the majority of its members for over twenty years!) Certainly there is no presumption in the Act that those who apply to the Court should be made to show that they have exhausted such internal remedies as are available to all union members. On the contrary, the probability is that a stipulation of this kind, in a union rule-book, would be regarded as contrary to the 'guiding principles' of the Act. And in the case of attempts to use the Act to secure the disenfranchisement of an established union there are no clear criteria of what is to be regarded as legitimate grounds of complaint. The Act refers in very general terms to the need to argue that 'a particular section' of workers has not been 'adequately' represented – language which hardly reassures, if one wants to avoid fractionalisation. Moreover, the CIR, on considering such an application, is given very limited discretion. The presumption is that those who can provide the necessary number of signatures will be able, in the end, to demand a ballot – and the result of the ballot will be legally binding.

It would appear from this somewhat frightening procedure that the authors of this part of the Act either did not know how breakaway groups develop on the shop floor, or if they did, they do not care. They have done their best to provide a breakaways' charter. They have certainly presented every would-be dissident with a ready-made platform, an instant programme of action and a useful rallying cry. It is difficult to imagine any set of legal rules less likely to promote the stable and representative unionism the Commission wanted to see.

But even this is not all. It will be remembered that the supporters of the Act argued that stability would be reintroduced if the group of workers who worked the revocation procedures went on to join a more representative union, which would then be free to use the sole bargaining agency provisions of the Act on their behalf. Unfortunately we have to ask the question, what kind of organisation is likely to make use of these provisions?

Even without their present opposition to the Act and its institutions, well-established unions would not be likely to do so. Most established unions belong to the TUC, and if they are found recruiting among the dissident members of another TUC union they can be taken to the TUC Disputes Committee. Certainly action designed to take advantage of the procedures of the Act goes against the spirit and intention of the TUC's Bridlington rules. (Indeed, attempts to enforce Bridlington principles under the TUC's rules are now of doubtful legality in any case.) Of course, given the existence of the Act there may well be a substitute union available, even if it has to be formed by the leaders of the dissident group itself. But such an organisation will almost certainly be sectional in origin, local in character, and without administrative experience. If past examples are any guide, its subscription levels will be ludicrously low.

One of the first aims of such a group will surely be to obtain entry to the provisional register established under the Act. Unfortunately the requirements of the Registrar are very vague on this matter and appear to be easily satisfied. The Registrar must ensure that would-be organisations are 'independent' of employers and have 'power' over their own rules. The Act says nothing about the experience of their leaders, or their financial viability, or their level of subscriptions. The Registrar is not even allowed to refuse registration on the grounds that the union concerned is too sectionally based, or that there are already more than enough unions organising in its chosen area. As a result he has already recognised a large number of small, sectional organisations, most of which would never gain entry to the TUC as *bona fide* organisations.

If the Act continues to promote the cause of organisations of this kind it could well lead to a proliferation of multi-unionism and competition on the workers' side of the bargaining table that will make existing trade union structures look remarkably logical, simple and effective. Of course, the activities of the Registrar in this respect may be corrected somewhat by a more selective approach on the part of the CIR when considering applications for recognition, but this cannot be relied on. It is true that the CIR has very broad terms of reference in this respect, but it remains to be seen how they will be interpreted.

Finally it is doubtful whether the genuine conscientious objector to trade unionism is much helped by the Act – unless he is prepared to go all the way and seek his legal rights. The trouble is that in practice the older, more settled worker is reluctant to do this. What he wants is toleration from his workmates and good-humoured acceptance of the fact that he is 'a special case'. All the evidence we have suggests that this kind of tolerance is maintained and developed most easily where unions are not fearful of their security; i.e. where their right to the closed shop for the great majority of workers is formalised and recognised, and this fact is well known. The Act will not help in this respect. It ensures that the closed shop will be enforced by stealth, by means of work-group pressures and collective action of various kinds. This is not the atmosphere that generates toleration for the occasional 'odd ball' who really does have a deep conviction, usually of a religious kind.

In practice this problem arises most frequently when unions are moving towards a closed shop situation. (Before this stage is reached the non-member raises no serious threat to union security. After the closed shop has been established it is rare for individuals to develop genuine conscientious objections.) This means that the problem is essentially one of accommodating the legitimate demand for union security and protecting the rights of existing objectors during the move towards the closed shop situation. The most practical solution is the compromise known as a 'registration shop agreement'. Under this arrangement the employer agrees that in future new entrants will be required to become and remain union members, and in exchange for this concession the union agrees to tolerate the continued non-unionism of a number of specified individuals within the bargaining unit.

The attraction of this kind of solution for the union is that the existence of an effective form of union security arrangement has been recorded or registered with the employer. This takes care of the long-term position. It also means that the few genuine conscientious objectors within the bargaining unit can be allowed to remain, for they no longer constitute any real threat. They, on their side, merely have to give an undertaking that they will not campaign among other workers to seek to convert them to their view. (Unfortunately this kind of sensible, humane and eminently practical solution is an unfair industrial practice under the Act. In a subsequent chapter we shall suggest how it might form the basis of part of a new Act, which would also contain measures designed to promote the reduction of multi-unionism.)

THE ACT IGNORED

At this point in the argument the reader may object. It may be true, he will say, that you have demonstrated that there is a conflict between traditionalist theories and Donovan objectives which the Act does not overcome. It could be right to assume that if those provisions of the Act which are designed to further traditionalist aims are invoked in the way you suggest the result will be weakened union leadership, a flight towards informalism, fractionalised trade unionism and a growth of intolerance towards genuine conscientious objectors. But all this hangs upon the assumption that every employer or worker who can sustain a case before the NIRC or the Industrial Tribunals will hurry off and demand his full legal rights under the Act. Surely this is an unnecessarily apocalyptic view of events, which its authors never intended? Haven't they been at pains to point out that the Act is supposed to work more gradually, and that in any case access to the Courts only takes place after conciliation by the Department of Employment? Surely this will make a difference – might it not result in the Act being beneficial after all?

This is in many ways a fair point. In the last section the qualification, 'if the Act is used', was constantly made. Many trade unionists believed that the Act would never be used and if they do not believe this any more it is possible to argue that in the pages above we have relied on the assumption that it will be used repeatedly and extensively to make most of our points. Moreover, ministers and others have frequently stressed that they were looking for a general improvement in the overall tone of industrial relations to achieve most of their beneficial effects. As Robert Carr has said:

> We do not claim that law by its direct action will achieve all that is needed. Its chief benefit will be its indirect and cumulative effect in influencing the way in which employers and unions and individual workers think and act and do their business together.

> Law forms opinion and influences behaviour. The positive code of law does much more than to provide sanctions against

the transgressor; it is not a matter of compelling people. It puts on record the judgement of the community about what conduct is fair and reasonable.[8]

Of course, statements emphasising the slow impact of the law, which are now common among traditionalists, contrast strongly with many of their earlier views. In 1968, for example, a common traditionalist argument was that Donovan's proposals were too slow to make any immediate impact on Britain's strike problem. A short, sharp and salutary legal impact was said to be needed, if only to get things moving. But there are more important points to be made in answer to this growing emphasis on the long-term effects.

To begin with, can it really be said that the Industrial Relations Act merely 'puts on record the judgement of the community about what conduct is fair and reasonable'? We have argued that a large part of it consists of a complicated attempt to reconcile two very different views of the contemporary industrial relations situation and what needs to be done to solve it. We have argued that there are strong reasons for supposing that these two views cannot be combined together. Certainly we have demonstrated that they have led to a complex and difficult set of legal provisions, the precise consequences of which are impossible to determine in advance. No man can say how the eventual outcome that results from the Courts applying these provisions will be regarded by the community at large. What can be said is that so far their application appears to have caused more controversy than consensus.

More importantly, the view advanced by Robert Carr, on further reflection, appears to amount to nothing more than an assertion that the Act will have a better effect if it is hardly ever used. It is difficult to see why this should be so. If the effects of using the Act continuously are likely to be as stated in earlier parts of this chapter – i.e. if, on balance, they will be positively damaging to industrial relations – it is hard to see how it can come about that their less frequent use will have beneficial consequences.

And if the answer is that the mere *threat* of the Act's use could be beneficial, whereas it is agreed that its actual use is likely to be disastrous, once again it is difficult to follow the argument. This is really to suppose a situation in which unions behave as if they were constantly expecting actions for damages, even though such actions rarely occur. But in this case, surely, the harmful effects on their relations with stewards, on their willingness to enter into more formal agreements, on the growth of breakaway organisations and so on, will still occur. In other words, if the criticism of the Act's operation in practice outlined in this chapter has any force at all then the damage it is likely to inflict on industrial relations in general and bargaining reform in particular, is not dependent upon the parties actually taking each other to court. Rather, it depends upon the ever-present threat of legal sanctions which the authors of this view themselves hope will continue to exercise what Robert Carr rightly terms an 'indirect and cumulative effect'.

To illustrate our point, let us suppose that very few actions are brought before the courts and that unions are only rarely held liable for the unfair industrial practices – which may well be the case. Let us also assume (and it would seem to be highly probable at the present time) that no unions sign legally enforceable collective agreements and that the government does not seek to impose them upon the two sides. Let us further suppose that firms collaborate with unions to ensure that post-entry and pre-entry closed shops continue in existence, although on the basis of informal understandings, as they have done in the US and most European countries, where these arrangements are also against the law. Finally, let us also suppose that despite the revocation procedures few breakaway unions develop and those that do are discouraged by employers and fail to obtain recognition. All these things may well happen. But even if they do it is difficult to see how this kind of development is supposed to count as a proof that the Act is working well. It is also difficult to see how this sort of farce is supposed to aid the process of bargaining reform.

What this will mean, at best, is that the provisions of the Act have been forgotten, so that the parties may be able to continue to work towards Donovan-type reforms as if the Act had never

75

existed. Of course, this optimistic prognosis may come about – in individual firms and plants. The interest of both sides in extending and reforming the scope and content of collective bargaining is now very considerable – as we shall show in chapter Five. It may well be that it will be able to override the snares and pitfalls placed in its way by the 1971 Industrial Relations Act. But even if this is the case, as we must hope, what a judgement it would be on the authors of the Act. To have begun by seeking to square the circle – to reconcile restraint with reform – merely to find that in the end reform only continues in spite of what you have done, because nobody in industry is interested in your proposals for restraint!

In any case, it is our submission that this is too risky a hope. Those who remain convinced that bargaining restraint and responsible trade unionism hold the key to future progress in industrial relations are entitled to continue to make the case for a still more draconian Act – so long as they accept that what they propose has little or no connection with the aims of bargaining reform and the promotion of more efficient management. The rest of us must surely think again about the kind of legal framework we need to assist these objectives in a more positive and comprehensive way.

Our argument is that this re-examination is urgent and necessary today if the forces making for reform in industry are to be rallied and focused on worthwhile objectives. We also consider that the best possible basis for such a reappraisal is the original analysis of the Donovan Commission. Chapter Five sets out to provide this reappraisal.

Notes

1 Lord Devlin, *Sunday Times*, 6 August 1972.
2 Donovan Research Paper 10, op. cit.
3 TUC Handbook on the Industrial Relations Act, TUC, 1970, p. 19.
4 Ibid., p. 21.
5 Ibid., p. 22.
6 Ibid., p. 22.
7 Donovan Report, p. 162.
8 Speech to Conservative Party Annual Conference, Brighton, October 1969.

5. The limitations of Donovan

'We do not think that the shortcomings of our existing industrial relations are due to malice or moral weakness on the part of employers, managers or trade unionists. They are primarily due to widespread ignorance about the most sensible and effective methods of conducting industrial relations, and to the very considerable obstacles to the use of sensible and effective methods contained in our present system.'

The Donovan Report, p. 51

'The job to be done, therefore, was educational, beginning with the Donovan Report itself, and subsequently to be carried on by the new Commission. When managers and trade unionists saw that current ideas about industrial relations were out of touch with reality, and had become a prop for outworn institutions, they would be ready to carry out the reforms that were needed.'

H. A. CLEGG[1]

THE ARGUMENT SO FAR

The earlier chapters of this book have sought to trace the assumptions and intellectual roots of the 1971 Industrial Relations Act. It has been shown to be an attempt to preserve traditionalist objectives while taking into account reformist aims. The conclusion reached is that these contradictory aims cannot be achieved, even though the Act pretends that they can. To the extent that the provisions designed to promote bargaining restraint and responsible trade unionism are taken note of, let alone used, they are likely to discourage moves in

77

the direction of bargaining reform and the range of objectives advocated by the Donovan Commission. The most we can hope for is that the forces of reform will prove strong enough to overcome the obstacles which the traditionalist parts of the Act place in their path.

All this is not to say that other parts of the Act may not result in some improvements. Workers are less likely to be unjustly dismissed because of the Act. The occasional abuse of union authority may be prevented by application of the 'guiding principles'. The CIR will probably publish carefully considered and wise recommendations for dealing with a range of industrial problems, even though its involvement with many of the most misguided parts of the Act (e.g. the revocation provisions) is bound to affect their acceptability. It is even possible to argue that sometimes the threat of legal action, and more importantly, the need to submit to conciliation before gaining access to the courts, may on occasion result in acceptable compromises. Most important of all the fact that there is an Act at all has focused the attention of top management on the need to have a policy for industrial relations, and much good has already resulted from this development.

Our position is not that no benefits can possibly come from the 1971 Industrial Relations Act. It is rather that the good that results is sometimes fortuitous, often achieved in spite of its other intentions, and that more progress could be made more easily in all these directions if the Act were purged of its counter-productive traditionalist objectives. The rest of this book assumes that this case has been proved, and goes on to consider its implications.

It begins with a re-examination of the assumptions and proposals of the Donovan Commission, with a view to answering the question: how far do they provide an adequate basis for thinking through an alternative set of policies which could find ultimate expression in a different legal framework? It is suggested that the first question to be answered is perhaps the most fundamental of all: What should be the reformer's basic attitude towards trade unionism?

WHERE DONOVAN WAS RIGHT

Donovan contains no general statement concerning the nature of trade unionism and its role in contemporary society. But the Commission makes it evident that it does not subscribe to conventional traditionalist views. As has been seen, traditionalists from the time of the 1869 Erle Commission have tended to assume that unions were in some meaningful sense culpable for the disturbance of what would otherwise be a broadly satisfactory state of affairs. This may be because they subscribe to the *agent provocateur* theory of union leadership. (This assumes that strikes, restrictive practices and inflationary wage increases arise largely because union leaders 'foment trouble' amongst basically moderate workers.) It could be because they give more weight to the *irresponsible* theory. (This argues that union leaders ought to be able, as a public duty, to direct and channel members' grievances and claims in a way that is thought to be moderate and responsible by the supporters of the theory.) It could be for some other reason. The point is that whatever set of assumptions are used, the traditionalist in practice applies essentially quietist criteria towards union leadership and organisation. If unions will not adopt these criteria themselves, laws must be found which force them to do so.

Whereas the traditional view looks for passivity and acquiescence on the part of a union and its members, the Donovan Commission saw active participation by workers in the determination of the conditions of their working lives as a crucial objective. And just as the traditionalist bases his search for passivity and acquiescence on an assumption of a basic harmony of interest between management and worker, so Donovan assumed a wider area of real and potential conflict of interest, stressing the need for management to take the initiative to find ways of adjusting and accommodating to the problems that will arise once workers become aware of the true situation and join trade unions.

The emphasis in Donovan is not upon using the unions to subdue the workers, but rather to help them to focus their demands on positive and achievable objectives. Unions are seen as the essential brokers of shop-floor power, the necessary formulators and adjusters of work-group demands. It is because there are unions, and workers and ex-workers can be found to run them, that there is a possibility that the mass of employees may be able to participate productively in determining what happens in the firm.

It is worth noting that this view of trade unionism does not involve the belief that union leaders can do no wrong. They can fail to present the true issues to their members. They can ignore their demands and be responsible for a wide variety of incompetent decisions and non-decisions. But in the end, if the challenge of the shop floor is to be focused towards positive and achievable objectives, union leadership must be allowed to respond to what it hears coming from below. Otherwise it is of no use to anybody.

It should be obvious by now that the writers of this book subscribe broadly to these views. They seem to us to be self-evident from the nature of trade unionism. (They are also, incidentally, supported by virtually every serious work devoted to the study of industrial relations, in this country and elsewhere.) Because of this we also feel that Donovan was broadly right to focus on the range of factors which have combined to produce a relatively unstructured and chaotic manifestation of work-group power in the British system of industrial relations.

Most of the current problems of British industrial relations are linked to defects in bargaining arrangements. Donovan's examples of the conflict between the 'pretences' of the formal system and the 'realities' of the shop floor could be extended and developed in many instances.

The Commission was right in arguing that the shift of power to the work-place cannot be reversed, or contained, within a reformed formal system operating at industry level. (Indeed, to judge from recent unemployment figures the power of the informal system to produce strike losses, inflationary pay settlements and so on, does not appear to decline notably even when wartime and post-war employment levels are significantly reduced.) It was therefore also broadly right to look for other ways of dealing with these problems. It was also wise to seek the answer in a new form and style of bargaining involving a different level of management, which would allow these problems to be tackled through the development of jointly agreed rules.

One of the crucial blindnesses of the traditionalist approach has always been to confuse rule observance with rule enforcement. Men tend to observe the rules they respect, and they respect above all rules that work. In industrial relations this means the rules that are supposed to deal with disputes, grievances and claims, as well as the rules and orders that management issues to get things done. In a work situation where it is well known that nothing is done 'by the rule-book' rule-making and rule observance becomes a joke. Only fools and toadies observe such rules. (It becomes accepted that if you want to solve a problem you don't go to the foreman. It is universally agreed that nobody takes any notice of the stopwatch. Nobody can remember the last time anybody saw a copy of the works' rule-book.) In such a situation it is impossible to make anyone believe that the only rule that should be observed is the one that says you ought not to take strike action until you have exhausted the procedure. And to be told, at this point, that it will in future be enforced by law only makes matters worse.

Donovan realised all this, and wanted to introduce more 'order' and rule observance. The extension of the scope and the transformation of the style of collective bargaining were seen as a way of agreeing on joint rules that had a chance of being observed – because they would be seen to work. There can be little doubt that in many instances the best point at which to seek to insert joint rule-making is at the individual factory or plant. At these levels one can take into account variations between different firms with respect to size, management structure and policies, technology and market situations, and thereby provide a framework for industrial relations which is tailor-made to suit the requirements of the individual establishment.

Prime responsibility for initiating moves towards factory and company agreements was also rightly placed with senior management. They are the only people who can take effective action to develop proposals for dealing with redundancy, discipline and so on. The invasion or circumscription of managerial prerogatives that an extension of bargaining scope on this scale requires must be agreed to by top-level management. They also have to understand why the new framework of joint rules has to become embodied in more precise and formal agreements designed to introduce a more consistent set of responses on management to all levels. But if the Commission was right in all this, where, if at all, was it wrong?

WHERE DONOVAN WAS WRONG

Three obvious criticisms can be made of the Donovan analysis. First, it oversimplified what was involved in introducing bargaining change. Second, it underestimated the legitimate conflict that could arise on the way. Third, it advanced an alternative structural model that was itself too simple to be applied universally. Once these obvious and somewhat superficial criticisms have been dealt with it is possible to see how they occurred, and thus get to the root of what needs to be done to develop the Donovan analysis in a way that fits our contemporary situation.

Perhaps the most frequent example of the Commission's tendency towards oversimplification lies in the fact that it so often wrote as if all that was required to transform British industrial relations was a once for all adjustment between the formal and the informal system. In its own words: 'What is of crucial importance is that the practices of the formal system have become increasingly empty, while the practices of the informal system have come to exert an ever greater influence . . .'[2] In effect, the Commission seemed to be saying that the process of reform amounted to a single major break with the past, rather than a continuous process of adaptation and change. In other words, all that is needed is a new and better arranged formal system which makes rule observance possible, unlike existing arrangements which effectively prevent rule adherence even where this is what the parties themselves are trying to achieve.

In fact, studies undertaken since the Commission reported indicate that the process of maintaining an adequate and observable bargaining structure is a complex and never-ending one.[3] A wide variety of external factors can disturb the effectiveness of a new pay structure. New products and processes can create different kinds of grievances and disputes that need to be handled in a different way. Plants can change and their markets can decline. Companies may move their location or alter their management system. All these developments and many more like them produce problems that test established bargaining arrangements. But even without these events, the workers themselves develop new demands and aspirations, which the existing bargaining system is not equipped to deal with. The Commission overlooked the need for techniques designed to monitor all such developments – so that at least management and unions remain aware of them, and are able to consider how the existing framework of rules should be adapted to cope.

Then, again, the Commission oversimplified when it implied, in the words of the quotation that heads this chapter, that most of the shortcomings of the present system were due to un-thinking custom, or 'widespread ignorance'. This suggests that anyone can conduct a successful experiment in bargaining reform, and that the problem, as Clegg suggests, was seen primarily as one of an 'educational' lag.

Of course, a lot depends on what is meant by education. Successful bargaining reform usually involves a training exercise of some kind, where stewards and supervisors are taught the meaning and application of the new agreements. It also depends, in its inception, on the awareness of top management that something needs to be done. It is possible to argue that education, in its widest sense, contributes to this process. But in between these levels, and in the case of those who will take prime responsibility for developing and negotiating the new system, what is needed much more is commitment, patience and experience. On the management side in particular, a major reform of pay structure, or the introduction of a new disciplinary code and procedure, involves a great deal of work and a considerable deployment of resources. It also often involves working through bargaining priorities and the industrial relations implications of all kinds arising from other management decisions. This can involve months of preparation before bargaining can even begin.

But the quotation at the head of this chapter also illustrates a further weakness in the Commission's analysis – the tendency to assume that 'employers, managers or trade unionists' would all agree on what needed to be done, once 'widespread ignorance' had been dealt with. The assumption was that there were likely to be no major differences of opinion between the parties on the precise content of bargaining reform. Again the findings of studies in firms where attempts to move in Donovan directions have been tried do not support this view.[4] On the contrary, it was found that serious disagreements usually arise between unions and management during the course of bargaining reform, and they affect each one of the four dimensions of bargaining structure – i.e., the *level* of bargaining, the *scope* or subject matter of bargaining, the size of the bargaining *unit* and the degree of *formality* required.

And disagreements are not always of the same kind. Usually management wants to lift the level of bargaining, but sometimes it is the unions that are arguing in this way for reasons of 'wage parity'. Normally it is management that is reluctant to slide forward the frontier of joint regulation, but occasionally the unions resist – as in the case of management proposals for the joint application of disciplinary rules. For the most part it is management that wants to increase the size of the bargaining unit, but the idea can come from shop stewards who see it as a chance to apply common standards. Very often the resistance to formalisation comes in the first instance from stewards, but they may well be in favour of formalisation in respect of shop steward facilities.

Unfortunately, the Donovan Report says very little about any of these problems, or how to overcome them. It is written as if men of good will on both sides are more or less bound to discern the ideal bargaining structure once it is pointed out to them by the Commissioners. Of course, this is not the case. Hard bargaining and judicious compromise is required before an agreed and mutually acceptable framework can emerge in any individual case. But this is so with all worthwhile reforms.

When one turns to the third criticism of Donovan, the suggestion that the Commission advanced an over-simple structural model that was not capable of general application, it is necessary to be careful about the kind of criticism that is justified. The Commission never claimed that its analysis of the two systems in conflict was directly applicable throughout industry, though it could be criticised for not stating the precise extent of its relevance. It offered few figures and no detailed estimates of the extent to which various industries and firms were affected by the 'two systems' conflict. In its defence, however, it should be pointed out that the case for bargaining reform does not fall because of this. It is certainly fallacious to suggest that *all* the Commission's comments on defective bargaining structures depend upon the extent to which the 'two systems' conflict is both universal and chronic.

It also had nothing to say about areas where its 'two systems' analysis did not apply – for example parts of the public sector that were suffering from low levels of management, or inadequate pay structures, or the ineffective use of labour. What the Commission failed to do was spend as much time on the solution of these problems as it did on those that arose in areas where the conflict between the two systems was chronic and intense. Donovan may have been right to suggest that where there is a high degree of conflict of this kind, 'formal', 'comprehensive' and 'ordered' agreements can be a useful tool for dealing with the problem. But it does not necessarily follow from this that other bargaining systems are not also in need of more widespread written agreements, or that they too would not benefit from introducing bargaining at the level of plant or factory. There is certainly no case for assuming that these reforms are only appropriate, or useful, to the extent that a given bargaining system suffers from a conflict between industry-wide agreements and shop-floor settlements.

D

Having described the way in which the Commission over-simplified and underestimated the problem involved in bargaining reform it should be obvious why it did so: it was aware, perhaps too much aware, of the case being made by the traditionalists at the time. It felt that if it was to provide an effective and easily understood alternative to the traditionalist case it had to be seen to be dealing with the same problems in a way that was equally direct and almost as easy to understand. Given the need to answer and demolish a defective but deceptively simple case, those who wrote the Report naturally felt that there was a limit to the details and complications that could be allowed to enter into the argument. If the alternative was a simple legal model it had to be answered by an institutional concept that was fairly easy to comprehend, defined in a way that did not stress too bluntly the need to modify to fit different circumstances and situations.

This understandable, perhaps inevitable development led to four further limitations on the scope and depth of the Donovan analysis which we seek to remedy in the next chapter:

1 The Commission did not consider at any length the nature of the shop-floor challenge which its institutional reforms were designed to accommodate and structure.
2 The Commission failed to discuss the other pressures operating on contemporary management which in practice limit and condition the responses it is able to make to this challenge.
3 Largely as a consequence of failing to undertake both the tasks set out above, the Commission did not spell out what was involved if it decided to follow the general approach it suggested in relation to the shop-floor challenge.
4 In the absence of a sufficiently wide and detailed analysis of the problem, the Commission naturally proposed a series of reforms and services that were themselves insufficiently ambitious and far-reaching. It also failed to point out how far what it suggested was likely to be influenced by events outside the industrial relations system.

Notes

1 H. A. Clegg, *The System of Industrial Relations in Great Britain,* Rowman and Littlefield, 1972, p. 454.
2 Donovan Report, p. 37.
3 See Department of Employment Manpower Papers No. 5, *The Reform of Collective Bargaining at Plant and Company Level,* HMSO, 1971.
4 Ibid.

6. Management by agreement

'The challenge that unions presented to management has, if viewed broadly, created superior and better-balanced management, even though some exceptions must be recognised ...'

'If one single statement were sought to describe the effect of unions on policy-making it would be: "they have encouraged investigation and reflection". Some unions are in fact only a slight check on management; other unions run the shop. But whether union influence is weak or strong, it always tends to force management to consider the probable consequences of its proposed decisions and to adjust those decisions accordingly.'

SUMNER H. SLICHTER, JAMES J. HEALY and
E. ROBERT LIVERNASH[1]

The aim of this chapter is to show that the conflict between the two systems stressed in the Donovan Report reflects a more basic conflict in contemporary industrial society. In the following section the conflict is analysed in terms of a double challenge now facing British management. In a further section it will be shown that the one effective way of meeting these pressures and adjusting to them is by an extension and transformation of the processes of collective bargaining, here termed 'management by agreement'. The changes in management and union behaviour that this would involve are discussed and analysed, and in a further section a new form of negotiation is suggested which would help encourage and implement the ideas behind management by agreement. The final section stresses that what is proposed is not in any sense a form of workers' control – though it may be regarded as part of a programme for extending workers' participation in management, and advancing the cause of industrial democracy.

88

THE DOUBLE CHALLENGE TO MANAGEMENT

Donovan's analysis of 'two systems' in conflict should be approached from the viewpoint of its impact on the average British manager. Here it takes the form of two opposing pressures. The first type has been rightly termed by Allan Flanders as the 'challenge from below' – by which is meant the demands made on management by an increasingly self-conscious and articulate labour force demanding its rightful share of power in industry.[2] As Flanders has also pointed out, the 'challenge from below' reflects wider social and economic developments in society generally. It is partly a reflection of present-day values which are critical of all kinds of authority – from the family to the state. In industry this means that an increasing number of workers of all degrees of skill feel that traditional authoritarian power structures are no longer acceptable, even when tempered by the most benevolent forms of paternalism. Indeed most workers are nowadays prepared to criticise all aspects of management performance and are unwilling to grant to those in authority any form of unquestioning obedience. They have developed their own standards of what constitutes efficient management and are not prepared to accept the legitimacy of decisions they regard as foolish or unnecessary. They also have their own norms and expectations against which to test and evaluate the treatment they receive and the adequacy of established wages and conditions. They are no longer willing to accept that any management is entitled to dismiss and punish without justification or explanation. Moreover, their standards concerning what constitutes a 'reasonable' wage or a proper degree of job security are themselves affected by the rising level of expectations and standards in society generally. This means that management decision-taking processes, in so far as they affect employees, are subject to constant criticism in a number of ways. Behaviour that was previously acceptable increasingly becomes grounds for deeply felt grievances. Groups that have habitually taken orders without question begin to expect to be consulted before changes are made affecting them.

At the cost of repeating a point it is essential to understand that this development is rooted in the hearts and minds of workers; it has not been planted there by devious or malevolent trade unions. It does, however, present trade unions with unrivalled opportunities, but only if they are prepared to observe the conditions that must be met for these to be realised. Trade unionism represents a convenient and increasingly relevant response to many of the demands and aspirations that workers now feel. It appears to provide both a means of satisfying more economic and materialistic aims and a way of challenging established authority at the place of work. And the attitudes which most new members bring to union membership are predominantly instrumental – they join in much the same spirit as customers enter a newly opened super-market; to sample the goods and see if their needs can be met more effectively by granting it their custom. Of course, no trade union can function effectively if all its members adopt an entirely instrumental attitude towards the organisation; it depends on the cement of common loyalty and trust that union officials and activists seek to engender and preserve. But they know full well that nowadays these feelings are not easily aroused and maintained. Unions can no longer command unquestioning loyalty, any more than employers or governments. It would be remarkable if the situation were otherwise.

Fortunately, for the union as well as management, there is usually a minority of the workforce for whom union membership and activity can come to mean something more. For the more active and reflective the union offers the prospect of group solidarity, participation in a form of voluntary effort that is more than the sum of its parts, and the possibility of work that demands real and immediate sacrifices in terms of time and money; a task that carries with it the prospect of its own rewards, mainly in the form of an increase in social status and the chance to fulfil a new and influential role at the place of work.

Most managers with any experience of trade unionism will readily admit that some of their best workers have been attracted by the opportunities for responsibility and service inherent in this aspect of union activity, and that these are the reasons why they become and remain shop stewards. They know that it is only because such people exist that unions are able to establish stable membership in their firm. They also realise that experienced and devoted stewards are their best guarantee of consistency so far as shop floor demands are concerned. Like the union officials described in the last chapter, they would be the last to deny the need for stewards to conform (in the end) to the demands of the shop floor, for they also realise that for stewards such behaviour constitutes the basic ingredient of their continued influence and respect.

What they look for are representatives who accurately reflect the more deep-seated and permanent aspirations and priorities of their members; men and women who know how to judge and articulate them in a way that management can understand and come to terms with. As Slichter, Healy and Livernash put the point in the quotation from their classic study of the impact of collective bargaining on American management which heads this chapter, management relies on the union to put the workers' point of view in a way that enables it to 'consider the probable consequences of its proposed decisions' and, if necessary, 'to adjust those decisions accordingly'.

Partly because efficient management in a modern company is a cooperative effort (where it helps if those who have to take decisions know how they are likely to be received), the union's role in encouraging 'investigation and reflection' is not necessarily resented or resisted. As the same authors go on to point out, the challenge that unions present can help to create 'superior and better-balanced management', given certain conditions. One of the essential conditions for many British firms was of course spelled out by the Donovan Commission, which stipulated that there must be an effective framework of rules for structuring and eliciting union demands and management responses. What Donovan failed to do was to discuss how certain other factors are making it progressively more difficult for even the most enlightened and well-meaning management to respond to union demands, even where the Donovan conditions are met. These factors constitute the second challenge now facing British management.

Flanders coined an illuminating image – the 'challenge

from below' – to characterise the increasing pressures that play on management as a result of the revolution in worker expectations. What has to be noted is that from management's viewpoint one of the most significant features of this 'challenge from below' is that it originates essentially *within* the enterprise. It is true that outside organisations such as unions have a part to play in focusing its impact, but they too are largely dependent on the ability and influence of workers within the firm to carry over their message and transmit their reactions to impulses that originate within the factory gates. In this sense an alternative term for the challenge from below might be the *challenge from within* – for there is also a growing *challenge from without* that we must now describe.

In recent years many managers have become increasingly aware of a complex of economic, technological and institutional pressures that appear to them to originate largely outside the firm. One of the most pressing of these is, of course, the growth of increasingly sophisticated and effective competition in the product market – which tends to have an increasingly international aspect. Another derives from the pace and complexity of technological change and innovation, which often produces and encourages the forces of product competition itself. A further pressure derives, paradoxically enough, from developments which are outside the firm but also within, in that they are rooted in management – in the broadest sense of the term. Here we refer to the growing development of the science and study of management; resulting in a bewildering variety of new management techniques and decisions which modern managers are expected to keep up with. There are also the activities of finance houses and others who set out to supply capital of various kinds to businessmen, together with the network of related institutions that nowadays claim to furnish various kinds of advice and guidance to investors and would-be investors. Doubtless their activities are profitable to those who own them, and they may even be useful to the public at large and the capital market in particular. Nevertheless, to many managers these activities pose a potential threat, which can end in either a redirection in managerial autonomy or a successful take-over bid. (But of course take-overs and mergers do not arise as a result of capital market transactions. The search for product integration and technological supremacy poses constant threats of this kind as well.) Finally, there are the increasingly important and apparently wayward activities of government. Economies are squeezed, or expanded, often with the briefest of warnings. Prices are pegged, or raised, by decisions to devalue or 'float', without any warning at all. New taxes are introduced and old taxes are discontinued – often in ways that make it impossible to calculate their likely effect on short-run costs or long-run demand for the product.

For us the most important thing to note about these and many other similar developments is that they all tend to produce the need for a series of changes within the enterprise itself. New products or processes are required; there is a search for better systems of management control or budgeting, improved methods of costing or investment appraisal, and improved patterns of purchasing, manufacturing and sales activity. Each and every one of these changes may, in its turn, challenge established patterns of work group behaviour. New wage systems may be required to fit more effectively the demands of new technologies. Different systems of work may be needed, involving shift patterns that affect both earnings and working hours. Established skills may no longer be needed. Existing plants and offices may become unproductive or obsolete.

Given the growth in the pressure and complexity of this challenge from without it might be natural to expect a general re-assertion of authoritarian styles of management. After all, managers are only human. Like the captain of a ship, or the pilot of a plane, they see stormy weather ahead. More and more quick decisions will be required, and some of them will be hard to take. There ought surely to be an overwhelming conviction arising in management that now is not the time to argue, explain, compromise or negotiate. '*If people want the ship to continue to stay afloat*', they might be expected to say, '*they will have to be prepared to take orders – my orders*'. Sometimes this feeling does become uppermost in the minds of individual managers – especially if they are facing well-entrenched trade unionism of a particularly militant and apparently unreasonable kind. But to us the remarkable thing is that such attitudes are not more common than they are in Britain today. And it is important that we should try to explain why this is so.

The most obvious reason is, of course, the growing strength and pervasiveness of the challenge from within. Managers know that the pursuit of what might be termed a 'hard line', insisting on their so-called 'managerial prerogatives', would involve them in using their economic power to the full. Strikes would result not merely from unusually high wage demands or other workers' claims, but also from the constant attempts of managers to win back the power they thought they needed to deal with the external threat. Naturally trade union leaders will assert that it is only the power of organised labour that prevents this from happening, but there are three other factors at work. First, managers today are not entirely unaffected by the more permissive and critical climate that is affecting society generally. This means that they are unsure of the legitimacy of a form of authority that is based on opposition to all forms of questioning and challenge from below. To an increasing number it does not seem reasonable to suggest that workers ought always to be willing to accept management's view of what is best for them. To do so assumes a degree of importance and far-sightedness on the part of management which many managers would not wish to lay claim to. It also suggests that management can usually guarantee to protect those who agree to conform to its orders. In the face of the growing challenge from outside many managers are no longer sure that this is possible. Sociologists would say that as a result many managers now subscribe to what they term a 'pluralistic' frame of reference.[3] This means, among other things, that they are uncertain how far they are justified in seeking to resist the growth of trade unionism – for example amongst white collar workers or supervisors. It also means that, where unions are recognised, there is a disposition to believe that outright battles designed to impose management's own definition of the needs of the challenge from outside are likely to be regarded as outdated and even immoral.

94

Second, and related to this development, modern managers are uneasily aware that certain aspects of the challenge from without menace their own position too. Take-overs and mergers can threaten executive job-opportunities and security even more directly than those of hourly paid workers. New technologies, or diversification, can threaten the demands for established management skills. Even new management techniques can produce managerial redundancy and obsolescence. For all these reasons an increasing number of middle managers are already trying to develop their own forms of collective action – including managerial trade unionism.

Finally, many managers are increasingly reluctant to react to the twin challenge by reverting to authoritarian styles and attitudes because they are coming to realise that many of the latest developments in technology and management science point in the opposite direction. It is not only that more capital intensive systems of production tend to increase the strategic power of workers if the conflict between them and management is pushed to a point where industrial action occurs. More important still, we think, are the developments that combine to make modern business an increasingly co-operative and inter-dependent activity, where efficiency and flexibility in the face of the growing demands of the external environment depend on the maintenance of effective group inter-action through the performance of a series of related tasks. Most students of management studies now agree that the most appropriate management style in circumstances of this kind is participative, even democratic. Managers are encouraged to discuss problems and potential decisions with their subordinates, and to encourage this process at all levels within the enterprise. They are also encouraged to delegate authority wherever and whenever possible, within the confines of an agreed corporate plan.

Very few firms have so far appreciated how to fit their relations with trade unions into this corporate plan, in a similarly participative and productive way. The existence of the climate that so often surrounds and informs the development and application of corporate plans within management itself

95

is a factor militating against the re-assertion of more traditionally authoritarian management responses. Most British managers are uneasily aware that there is no way out for them in this direction. Somehow they have to find a better way of reconciliating or dealing with the twin demands that face them.

MANAGEMENT BY AGREEMENT

Once one rejects attempts to insist on the right of management to decide unilaterally there can be only one alternative way forward; authority must be shared with workers through an extension of the area of joint regulation. This is the essence of 'management by agreement'. We suggest that the conflicting claims made on the enterprise can best be adjusted and, so far as is possible, reconciled if an attempt is made to reach agreements with the representatives of the workers in a framework of jointly agreed rules that will specify and regulate the responses the firm makes to both the challenge from below and the challenge from outside. In practice this would entail a transformation of the normal processes of collective bargaining so that collective agreements are developed which cover subjects and areas of management decision-taking that extend well beyond those proposed by the Donovan Commission. This would entail a circumscription of existing unilateral rights and customs on both sides of the bargaining table, but in exchange a broad area of agreement would exist on the way the firm should be managed to meet the problems it faces.

One way of symbolising this concept would be to say that within a system of management by agreement there would no longer exist any area of management decision-taking where management itself could claim an absolute and unilateral right to resist union influence in any form. In other words there would no longer be any room for a doctrine of employer 'reserved rights' or 'managerial prerogatives'. At the moment most managers assume that there is some kind of area or 'sacred garden' of management prerogatives which unions must never be allowed to over-run – though they are becoming increasingly hazy about its boundaries. Thus most managers still refuse to discuss the principles on which foremen are selected with shop stewards, and would regard investment decisions or pricing policy as matters of no concern to trade unions. The steward, or union official, who asks why it was thought necessary to raise the return to shareholders this year, is likely to be told that this is none of his business.

Under a system of management by agreement a response of this kind would no longer be in order. Unions would have the right to seek to influence management policy in *any* area – including such matters as investment decisions, rates of profit, management salaries and so on. Of course it does not follow from this that the management would be committed to revealing confidential information, or that it be forced to agree with the union on what should be done. (This is not the case when unions make demands in respect of other areas of management decision-taking, for example wage rates and working conditions. Why should it be assumed to be the case if joint discussion and joint regulation are extended beyond these limits?) What management would be committed to is providing reasonable explanations for policy decisions in these areas. They would also be committed to listening to union criticism and pledged to doing their best to answer it.

More positively, the notion of management by agreement does involve the assumption that where possible agreements in any area ought to be recorded, as formal understandings. And even where proposals and criticisms do not emerge from discussion with union representatives, management ought to be trying to widen the area of joint regulation by initiatives of its own. Thus discussion of specific problems of wage anomalies and other disparities should be regarded as opportunities to raise general issues of relativities and differential between groups. Moreover, discussions of this kind should lead on to problems of pay structures and the relationship between this aspect of total costs and other factors. The influence of cost structures on liquidity problems should also be explored, just as the relationship between costs, profits and sources of finance ought not to be overlooked. All these factors are ultimately related to the ability of the firm to exploit and maintain existing and potential product markets. Success in these areas can be shown to be directly relevant to the ability of the firm to pay acceptable and competitive rewards to all its employees, including its managers.

Perhaps it should be stressed at this point that what is being proposed is not advanced as a device to divert the workers from their immediate objectives. It is not proposed as a management confidence trick, designed to lead shop stewards into debates about complex subjects which they will never quite understand. (The employer who embraces management by agreement with this aim in mind is bound to fail.) What is suggested can be justified on four related grounds, which are all directly connected to the complex of pressures that face firms today. First, management by agreement provides the only means of responding to the complex nature of the pressures that come from below. Second, it offers the best prospect of gaining agreement for the introduction and application of necessary change within the enterprise. Third, it provides a way of more effectively utilising the potentialities of the work-force itself. Fourth, it is only through the development of new forms of collective bargaining based on the notion of management by agreement that there is any hope of bringing home to workers the reality of the pressures that face the enterprise from outside. Each of these justifications needs to be developed separately.

In respect of the first it can be agreed that given the wide and general nature of the factors making up the challenge from below, nothing less will do. Workers, as we have seen, are nowadays prepared to criticise all aspects of management. The demands and claims they make on the modern enterprise stretch beyond the customary and traditional, and are fed by rising expectations, the collapse of authoritarian notions of legitimacy, and subservience in society at large. It is self-evident that if these claims on the enterprise are to be met, or even understood, the frontiers of joint decision-taking must be extended to meet them. One way of putting this point in a practical way is to say that it is now time to end what has been termed 'the money solution' in British industrial relations. By this is meant the tendency of both sides to assume that all demands and criticisms can be bought off or deflected if only people are given an opportunity to earn enough money. In the past the money solution has contributed to the militancy and obstinacy of many shop floor groups – most notably in the motor industry and the docks. Even today the assumptions on which it rests continues to dominate the responses of many managers in other industries – such as construction.

Management by agreement could be said to embody the opposite assumption; i.e. the view that it is in the interests of both sides to follow through the causes of all disputes and grievances (to discover how far they are rooted in wider and more far-reaching claims and criticisms), and a recognition that institutional mechanisms may have to be devised to deal with all the problems uncovered, even if they pose serious problems for management in terms of the maintenance of existing patterns of authority and power. Only in this way will it be possible to show that management has done its best to try to come to terms with all the forms taken by the challenge from below.

Second, and just as important, there is convincing evidence to show that most important internal adjustments that need to be made to meet the external challenge require the active co-operation of the workforce if they are to be surmounted effectively. Worker involvement and expertise are required if expensive new improvements in work routines, layouts, processes and products are to be implemented as intended. The road to greater productivity is littered with the production losses of management who failed to learn this elementary lesson; men who saw technical advance as a way of weakening or destroying well established methods of shop-floor control. The result has been that where workers have been prepared to agree to the introduction of new methods they have either consciously or unconsciously sabotaged their operation in their determination to maintain some degree of control over their own work environment.

What management by agreement implies is that management has to realise that *all* proposals for change ought to be viewed as opportunities for improving and extending techniques of joint control, principally through the medium of collective bargaining. It is necessary to point out that this is just as important where management believes that the changes proposed are designed to encourage worker participation and involvement in other ways. To illustrate the point with an example, studies have shown that as a result of the work of Hertzberg and others, the workers' sense of involvement and job satisfaction can be considerably improved by a suitable re-arrangement of work tasks, designed to improve the range of work done by individuals and semi-autonomous work groups.[4]

Various names have been given to different kinds of developments of this sort, including job rotation, job enlargement, job enrichment and so on. Linked to ideas of this kind are others that provide for improved systems of supervision, such as 'core group' techniques, or proposals for what are termed 'total involvement exercises', designed to raise work-group participation in deciding how changes shall be introduced.

What is not realised is how sceptical most workers are of the benefits likely to acrue to them from all experiments of this kind, and how far scepticism is fed by management's inability to grasp the connection between the new systems they propose, and established methods of collective bargaining. Workers are bound to be suspicious if changes are suggested which are not linked to their well tried techniques for influencing the job environment. This means that *all* proposals for work restructuring, or any other new idea, must first be raised through the normal process of negotiation. Moreover, their operation and impact should be fully discussed with union representatives, and the pace and method of their introduction should be regulated by new kinds of monitoring agreements, designed to ensure that shop stewards have a major role in deciding how they operate. Above all change must not be regarded (or appear to be regarded), as a way of undermining the realities of shop-floor influence.

The third justification for the approach advanced above referred to the even more widespread evidence of a connection between participative systems of decision-taking and the

release of potentialities for self-government and job-involve-
ment in ordinary work people. The best recent summary of this
evidence is contained in Paul Blumberg's book, *Industrial
Democracy: The Sociology of Participation.*[5] Summarising the
results of studies of many different kinds of experiments in a
wide variety of firms and countries. Blumberg says: 'There is
hardly a study in the entire literature which fails to demonstrate
that satisfaction in work is enhanced or that other generally
acknowledged beneficial consequences accrue from a genuine
increase in workers' decision-making power. Such consistency
of findings, I submit, is rare in social research.'

Considering why this should be so Blumberg concludes: 'It
is not really difficult to explain why participation "works";
it is almost a matter of common sense that men will take greater
pride and pleasure in their work if they are allowed to participate in shaping the policies and decisions which affect that
work.'[6]

Nowadays this commonsense notion would not be denied by
many progressive managers, and we have referred to their
awareness of the benefits to be derived from more participative
styles of decision-taking earlier in this chapter. What is not so
readily appreciated is that from the viewpoint of the organised
worker collective bargaining represents participation in its
most acceptable form.

Finally, management by agreement offers the best prospect
of establishing a formal link between the two challenges that
face British management today; and the most effective means
of bringing home to workers the extent to which their claims
are ultimately dependent upon the firm's ability to surmount
and exploit the challenges posed by the external environment.
This is not to say that as a result management will get employees to accept their definition of the situation; nor does it
mean that as a result they should expect to enjoy the sympathy
of their shop stewards. What is hoped is that by providing a
forum for joint discussion and decision the two sides will become
more aware of what is involved in attempting the process of
adjustment. What is hoped is that on the employees' side the
possession of a greater degree of influence will lead to a greater

awareness of the relationship between the claims they are making and other demands made on the enterprise, such as those of its customers, suppliers, etc. On the management side the hope is that as a result better solutions will be found to many problems, and that even where this is not the case the process of 'investigation and reflection' that Slichter, Healy and Livernash described will make them more sensitive to the likely reactions to their proposed plans from the workforce.

The next section advances the case for a new form of collective bargaining is advanced which will help to carry forward the frontiers of joint-regulation in a productive and acceptable direction.

THE DEVELOPMENT OF PREDICTIVE BARGAINING

So far this chapter has said little that many progressive managers would disagree with, at least in principle. Many would accept that there is no overwhelming reason why the frontier of joint-regulation bargaining should not be allowed to move forward, if this helps them with the task of adjusting to the twin pressures that face them today. Indeed, in a few instances known to us, managers have moved to the point where they are willing to discuss virtually any issue which employee representatives care to raise. However, this has usually been on an *ad hoc* and rather personal basis, and there has been little to show for it in terms of formal agreement.

The central aim of this form of negotiation would be to change the emphasis of bargaining from recriminations over the past to planning for the future. As a result the future would have to be jointly predicted and provided for in the agreements that resulted. For this reason we term this form of negotiation *predictive bargaining*.

It is still the case that far too much of the atmosphere around the bargaining table is rooted in the past. This is largely because most negotiation arises out of attempts to redress and adjust past grievances and complaints by one side or the other. As a result it is often dominated by defensive attitudes on the part of management – who are over-concerned to show that earlier mistakes made by one or another of their subordinates are not their fault, and, on the union side, this is matched by a desire to cultivate and keep fresh the memory of long-standing wrongs. As a result stewards often adopt an unproductive and irritatingly inquisitorial style which naturally annoys management. Moreover, such attitudes, once adopted, have to be justified outside the bargaining room. This does not help in the Board Room or on the shop floor.

We suggest that one way in which a more productive atmosphere might be generated would be if a link could be established between collective bargaining and corporate planning, by which is meant that process which attempts to relate the objectives of different aspects of the business to each other. It is true that many different procedures are followed under the name of corporate planning in different firms, depending on their size, business objectives, and the degree of sophistication of their management. Nevertheless in most firms of any size there is a corporate plan of some kind, even if it rarely has anything to do with what is happening on the shop floor.

In the corporate planning process those responsible for various aspects of the business usually begin by studying recent trends in their own areas of responsibility. From this analysis they develop potential or optimum targets for future expansion or development over a prescribed period of time. Corporate activity begins when these aims or objectives are placed side by side – to see how far they mesh in with each other. Thus production plans and future factor inputs have to be squared with anticipated market trends and sales objectives. These, in turn, have to be shown to be compatible with estimates of future financial resources and cash flows. Room then has to be found for innovation, product development and for a competitive rate of return on capital. Finally, it has to be agreed that the targets that emerge from all this are within the capacities of existing management.

Integrating industrial relations objectives into a process of this kind would have to begin with a joint appraisal by management and unions of the adequacy or otherwise of existing ways of doing things. Efficiency audits would be required concerning all the major aspects of what is sometimes called the 'wage-work equation' – i.e. all the factors governing the work people do for the pay they receive in a given firm; for example the payment system, methods of work structuring, or suggestions aimed at increasing job-mobility, etc. Targets of this kind would then be costed and attempts made to assess their relative contribution to other known aspects of the corporate plan.

Of course the unions would have to have time to consult their members on all these matters, and no doubt there would be disagreement between the two sides on priorities, costs and relative benefits. But when disagreement came it would at least occur after a thorough review of a range of alternatives and after a sustained attempt to reach a measure of agreement. Moreover, in the course of discussions unions would have access to the outline of other aspects of the corporate plan – so that they would be in a better position to evaluate their impact. They would also be free to suggest ways in which the plan might be altered, or adapted, to help to gain their agreement on its industrial relations aspects. Thus they might suggest that the pace of proposed innovation was too fast, or that its impact was too uncertain. Modifications might be proposed in production targets, or future manpower plans. Unions could take the view that their position would be made easier if only management would agree to revise its marketing objectives, or pricing policy, or diversify its products in a more labour intensive way. Objections could even be lodged against proposals to appoint individual managers to carry out certain parts of the corporate plan, or to the salaries they would be paid. (No doubt complaints would always be made about the allowances made for returns to capital and how best to measure them.)

Under this procedure management would not react to ideas and suggestions of this kind with horror, or shock. On the contrary, every attempt would be made to seek to meet the unions on all these points. As a result plants might not be closed down, or closed down so quickly. New markets might be tried, or new pricing policies introduced. Bonus issues might be abandoned and even different heads of departments might be appointed. For in the end the aim would be to reach agreement wherever and whenever possible on the broad lines on which the enterprise was to run.

And where agreement was not forthcoming, because one side or another could not carry their followers with them, or because, on balance, they felt that the other side had not offered them a concession sufficient to justify them abandoning a previous position; the customary rules of collective bargaining would still apply, each side would remain free to take what action it thought fit in the circumstances. But once again it could at least be said that every avenue towards agreement had been explored, and in a way that was likely to assist in the adjustment of the challenge from below to the challenge from outside.

But predictive bargaining would not end with the signing of agreements concerning the industrial relations aspects of the corporate plan. Wherever possible the agreements would contain provisions establishing a continuous link between the terms of the wage-work equation and other aspects of business performance. There is of course nothing new in this idea in itself. Every output bonus scheme that includes extra payments when output rises may be said to constitute such a link. But in recent years a number of novel schemes have been developed for 'plant-wide' or 'company-wide' bonuses that would appear to be rather more appropriate to the furtherance of wider corporate objectives. (These include ways of linking extra payments with the achievement of broad estimates of industrial relations success, such as those related to improvements in 'added value' or overall 'cost reduction'.)

Similar ideas of a more advanced kind have been advanced recently in Germany and elsewhere for ways of linking worker remuneration with the long-run capital growth of the business, sometimes termed 'capital growth' or 'share of prosperity plans'. For the most part these schemes are a great advance on old-fashioned profit sharing schemes, but it is arguable that they derive from similar aims and intentions.

More generally, and in conclusion, we would also like to see links established between the terms of the wage work equation and other kinds of corporate targets – both inside and outside the industrial relations system. But we think these links would be best discerned and forged during the period when 'first generation' predictive bargaining agreements were being monitored – i.e. during the period of their operation. This is one reason why predictive agreements would almost certainly always be signed for fixed periods – say one or two years. During such periods both sides would be able to assess their adequacy and acceptability, comparing relative failures and successes with targets established for other sectors of the business. When the time came for review both sides would be in a better position to assess the justifiability of arguments used by the other side. As a result it should be more likely that they would find it easier to agree on future targets during the next round of negotiations.

Finally, every effort should be made to involve workers on the shop floor in the actual execution of the agreed parts of the corporate plan, and to keep them informed about its progress. Under the broad umbrella of enabling collective agreements all kinds of experiments and innovations should be tried. These could involve areas of joint executive action, such as participative systems of job-assessment and promotion. It could include autonomous group control of work scheduling and quality control, together with the introduction of worker-based monitoring techniques designed to avoid the need for conventional supervision of work tasks.

THE LIMITS OF MANAGEMENT BY AGREEMENT

We have now completed our answers to three of the questions raised at the end of the previous chapter concerning the limitations in the scope and depth of the Donovan Report. This chapter has suggested a way of developing its analysis to a point where it is possible to deal with the double challenge now facing British management. At this stage it is necessary to sound a number of notes of warning and qualification.

What has been proposed above is not a system of workers'

control. It is a meaningful form of workers' participation in management, and taken together with various other proposals that follow in later chapters could be said to represent a programme for promoting industrial democracy. These proposals are not intended to challenge management's ultimate responsibility for running the enterprise. As in all forms of collective bargaining this remains intact. The implications of this point can perhaps best be made clear by following through the consequences of disagreement in more detail.

Once a matter is accepted as a fit subject for negotiation the parties are committed to try to reach a mutually acceptable way of dealing with it, if possible by means of a formal understanding or agreement that specifies the rules to be observed in future. Thus agreements on wage rates, or hours of work, or promotion principles, or the rate at which a given plant is to be run down, or new systems of work are to be introduced, regulates and limits what management can do in this field for the period that the agreement runs. But in all forms of negotiation there are bound to be failures to agree. What happens then is that once an agreed procedure has been exhausted both sides are free to act unilaterally. In the case of most of the new areas of managerial decision involved in predictive bargaining, a failure to agree would usually result in a management decision in the face of union opposition. The unions and their members would then have to decide what to do about this decision. One of the options would normally include the right to use unilateral collective action in the form of a strike.

This response would not be a common feature of predictive bargaining. And if it happened the chances are that more than one issue would be involved. Thus a strike might take place basically because agreement could not be reached on a wage issue, or a redundancy problem – though both sides would know that if agreement could have been reached on some other aspect of management decision-taking, such as future pricing policy, or promotion opportunities, or even marketing strategy, this might have been eventually avoided. In fact an exploration of these wider issues is likely to make a strike less likely rather than more probable, for it will help to bring into consideration

Management by agreement

factors which are capable of variation by one side or another, as against those that are genuinely beyond their control. It will also help to reveal what trade-offs will be required if agreement is to be reached in the end. Nevertheless it must be recognised that in principle the result of failing to agree on one or another of these issues could be the actual cause of a strike, designed to put pressure on management to change this aspect of policy.

The right of ultimate recourse to unilateral action on the part of either party is derived from a frank admission that there are major and at times irreconcilable differences between management and workers. Workers must have the right, in the end, to determine how far they are prepared to modify their demands as a result of taking into account what are essentially management problems. Similar rights must also be permitted to management, and the situation would not be basically very different if *all* managers and workers were employed in publicly owned industries. What we look for, and what we aim to provide, is a mechanism for dealing with these differences rather than a formula for apparently dissolving them. Recourse to industrial action will be a continuing feature of a reformed system of industrial relations; for this reason the next chapter contains proposals for improving the facilities for resolving and preventing strikes.

Finally, it must also be stressed that inherent in the notion of management by agreement is the assumption that both sides will be willing to change their bargaining habits. Unless this is possible what is being proposed here simply cannot work. On the management side what is suggested is time consuming. Much more effort will have to be put into thinking through the consequences of general business objectives and decisions on the workforce. There will have to be a far greater readiness to give reasons for what is done, and to ensure that these are consistent. Mistakes will have to be acknowledged more readily and a management style adopted which does not rely on assumptions of infallibility. For reasons advanced earlier, when discussing recent developments in management thinking, we see no reason to consider that requirements of this sort will inhibit management efficiency. On the contrary what they will mean is that more resources will have to be channelled into the industrial relations functions of management.

There will also have to be changes on the union side. It has been pointed out earlier how the extension of the frontier of joint regulation usually poses problems for trade unions. As shown, Donovan's proposals for more formal and precise plant and company agreements tend to circumscribe their ability to respond to day to day pressures; certain arguments are excluded, certain tactics ruled out. This process is bound to be taken further if unions join management in experiments in predictive bargaining. One way of suggesting what will be involved is to talk in terms of a more 'structured' union response. In effect this means that the challenge from below will have to be focused on a more carefully selected range of targets and directed at managers in a more precise and predictable way. And here again the key may well be the adoption of a system of fixed term agreements. Certainly the present tradition of 'open-ended' agreements that continue until one side or another gives notice that they wish to change them, is not really compatible with a move towards predictive bargaining. After all, if management is to be induced to open up new areas to discussion and agree to new subjects for joint agreement there must be a period in which management is allowed to get on with implementing what is agreed. Corporate plans cannot be changed overnight, and attempts to monitor and assess the impact of all aspects of the wage work equation on other parts of the business take a considerable time.

Again there is no reason to oppose the proposals advanced on this score. On the contrary, in the next chapter additional reasons will be given for favouring a move towards fixed term agreements on quite different grounds. However, it must be understood that moves of this kind will involve both union members and their spokesmen in new habits and patterns of behaviour. What has to be examined is how far these changes are likely to take place without external assistance and advice, and what problems are likely to arise if attempts are to be made to provide more assistance in this direction.

Notes

1 S. H. Slichter, J. J. Healy and E. R. Livernash, *The Impact of Collective Bargaining on Management*, the Brookings Institution, 1960, pp. 251 and 252.
2 Allan Flanders, *Industrial Relations: What is wrong with the system?* IPM, 1965, chapter 5.
3 See Donovan Report; Research Paper 3: *Industrial Sociology and Industrial Relations*, by Alan Fox, HMSO, 1966.
4 W. W. Daniel and N. McIntosh, *The Right to Manage*, MacDonald-PEP, 1972.
5 Paul Blumberg, *Industrial Democracy: The Sociology of Participation*, Constable, 1968.
6 Ibid., p. 123.

7. The case for constructive mediation

'Guidance by a third party to an acceptable accommodation is the essence of mediation . . . participation of a third party in a situation which is already given will be called 'tactical' mediation. 'Strategical' mediation consists, instead, of the structuring of the situation itself, of the creation of a favourable environment within which the parties interact. The purpose of tactical mediation is to bring existing nonviolent conflict between the parties to a mutually acceptable result so that there will be no need for it to become violent or to end in openviolent conflict by agreement or by transfer to nonviolent means. Strategical mediation aims instead at reducing the incidence of conflict and channeling it along nondestructive lines of development.'

CLARK KERR[1]

The notion of 'management by agreement' is an attempt to develop and extend the 'non-traditional' or Donovan view of what is wrong with our system of industrial relations. It focuses on bargaining reform rather than bargaining restraint. This chapter aims to describe how this programme of reform can best be advanced. It begins by considering a number of alternative possibilities, then demonstrates that the main emphasis should be placed on what is termed *constructive mediation*, by describing how it would differ from existing forms of mediation, and including a section on the limitations and defects of existing mediation services. Emphasis is placed on the need to overcome two features of existing services. First, their continued reliance on outdated notions of 'voluntarism'. Second, the growing tide of criticism that derives from the suggestion that government 'interference' has undermined the traditional 'independence' of the services. The final sections of the chapter describe how a more positive and independent form of mediation might work in practice.

THE OPTIONS AVAILABLE

Three different options immediately suggest themselves. First, one could decide that progress can only come by means of voluntary action by the parties based on education and the gradual spread of enlightenment. To some extent, it has been noted, the Donovan Commission took this view about its programme of reform. It stressed the importance of education and relied heavily on the influence of its report in dispelling 'widespread ignorance about the most sensible and effective methods of conducting industrial relations'. It is easy to see why it adopted this position, and there is much to be said for it. After all, meaningful and workable changes in bargaining structure depend, in the last resort, on management and union commitment to carry them through. As Clegg suggests in the quotation that heads chapter Five, very little can be done unless and until one or both of the parties come to accept that their current ideas are 'out of touch with reality' and 'a prop for outworn institutions'.

Those totally committed to this view will naturally assume that an outside agency – such as the government – can do little to help, except perhaps by subsidising the right kind of publicity; for example, studies of companies and unions that have successfully pioneered reform. But the limitations of this approach are only too easily stated. On the assumption that reform is in any way urgent it is open to the charge that the solution proposed is far too slow and offers no sure prospect of rapid advance. Moreover, in the case of movement towards management by agreement, it can also be said that the changes in bargaining attitudes and structures proposed are considerable, involving a difficult and complex process of adaptation on both sides. (What is suggested is, after all, more far reaching and time consuming than the reforms advocated by the Donovan Commission, and it is not assumed that there is any simple procedural model that can be easily applied to bring it into effect.) Given the nature of the pressures now operating on most managements and unions it is only reasonable to doubt how far they would have the necessary time and means to accomplish everything that needs to be done, if they were left to rely entirely upon their own resources.

Moreover, day-to-day pressure will be most intense in situations where reform is most needed – i.e. in firms where formidable pressures of external adaptation are combined with extremely strong shop floor organisation. Here both sides are naturally apt to become obsessed by the need to deal with continual short run demands and adjustments, rooted in past grievances and present threats. In this not uncommon situation it would seem that a decision to rely on the slow process of education would leave any government open to the criticism that it was not doing enough about the serious problems of industrial relations in Britain today. Indeed it was precisely considerations of this kind that were instrumental in paving the way for the 1971 Industrial Relations Act.

This brings us to the second option that must be considered; reliance on law. Both sides of industry could be compelled to engage in management by agreement by means of legal regulation. The difficulty is to think of any actual laws that would help. Of course we have already agreed that virtually all the proposals contained in the 1971 Act are likely to be counterproductive, but this is mainly because they are linked to contradictory aims derived from notions of bargaining restraint. It does not follow from this that more promising proposals cannot be invented. We are certainly not prepared to argue that there is nothing the law can do to promote management by agreement. On the contrary, the right kind of legislation can encourage moves in this direction. Thus the next chapter will suggest new legal provisions which could help to reduce the incidence of strikes. It will also be supporting an idea suggested by the Donovan Commission that needs to be developed and extended – i.e. its proposal that firms above a certain size should be obliged to register their agreements. A number of new proposals for legislation will also be suggested, but it is necessary, at this point, to stress that the use of the law in this field has very definite limitations for three related reasons.

First, if the law is to be used to promote bargaining reform then care must be taken to ensure that it does not deter the parties from assuming their own responsibilities. It should leave them an area of discretion and is probably most effective when it only attempts to exert indirect or general pressures. (Donovan's proposals for the registration of agreements are an example of this kind of indirect legal pressure.) Second, it is also important to ensure that any laws proposed for inducing certain types of action do not give rise to counter-productive secondary effects. (The 1971 Act's provisions for sole bargaining agencies are a very good example of this danger in practice.) Unfortunately the most obvious way to prevent this happening would involve making these provisions very direct and precise, thus leaving little scope for discretion and voluntary action. Third, and most important of all, the law finds it easiest to prevent established and easily discernible patterns of behaviour which the majority of citizens feel to be wrong. But this is not the nature of the problem. We want to induce positive acts and initiatives in new and untried directions, and – at least at their inception – the less they are publicised the better. All these considerations mean that in practice it would appear to be extremely difficult to think of many worthwhile proposals for advancing the cause of management by agreement by means of the law. We would therefore place our main emphasis on the third option, which must now be considered.

THE DEVELOPMENT OF CONSTRUCTIVE MEDIATION

If the practical reformer rejects exclusive reliance on the forces of enlightenment, because they are likely to be too slow, but nevertheless remains sceptical of the extent to which the law can help, he has only one avenue of influence left open to him. He must seek to create a network of public institutions designed to promote and further his chosen aims in a systematic manner. This 'middle way' to social and economic reform is, of course, very often used to deal with other complex and sensitive issues – for example in the area of race relations, and the expansion and control of higher education. It has the advantages of flexibility, diversity, and it can be easily combined with the encouragement of voluntary action and occasional legal reinforcement.

It is necessary to create a network of public institutions designed to promote the systematic reform and improvement of industrial relations and its more peaceful operation, a catalyst for change, and an agency which will also assist in the resolution of industrial conflict. The emphasis must be placed on conflict resolution, as well as bargaining reform, because, as was argued earlier, in its desire to over-simplify, the Donovan Commission seriously underestimated the extent to which industrial conflict would continue even within the most reformed and advanced system of industrial relations. Moreover, since the publication of its Report the volume of industrial conflict – measured in terms of workers involved in strikes, and working days lost – has considerably increased. Thus in the years considered by the Commission, the number of working days lost through strikes rarely exceeded four million. In 1972 nearly twenty-four million working days were lost as a result of strike action.

A range of inter-related and inter-dependent agencies would be capable of tackling *both* of these problems at the same time. Borrowing a term from Clark Kerr, whose comments about the role of third parties in industrial relations are quoted at the head of this chapter, the best 'umbrella' word to use to characterise the main aim of these proposed services is *mediation*. By mediation is meant, in his words, 'guidance by a third party to an acceptable accommodation'. It also helps to make use of his distinction between 'strategical' and 'tactical' mediation, and these are best performed as closely connected processes.

Strategical mediation, says Kerr, is concerned with more long-term improvements designed to 'structure' the collective bargaining situation. In effect it deals with the ground rules of bargaining, such as the changes in bargaining 'scope', 'forms', 'levels' and 'units' that the Donovan Commission wished to see. Strategical mediation should be seen as a major force assisting the introduction of the system of collective bargaining termed here management by agreement.

By tactical mediation Kerr means action 'within the existing rules' designed to produce accommodation – in other words, all forms of third party dispute resolution. In practical terms, in Britain, tactical mediation includes the work of independent conciliators and much of the activity of industrial Courts of Inquiry and Committees of Investigation – at least in so far as the members of these bodies are simply concerned with proposing ways of settling disputes within the broad framework of existing rules. It also covers most of the activities of arbitrators – who are usually expected to propose fairly short-run accommodations when the parties are unable to find them for themselves. On the other hand, tactical mediation does not cover the more far-reaching proposals of a body like the 1965 Devlin Committee on the Docks. For Lord Devlin and his colleagues went beyond the causes of a particular dispute and proposed a number of important general reforms in the structure and content of bargaining in the docks. That aspect of Devlin's work we would describe as strategical mediation.

Both forms of mediation may be said to advance common goals, and need to be made to work in mutually reinforcing ways. A term which symbolises the connection which should serve to link them is *constructive mediation*. A rapid and far-reaching extension of constructive mediation services could be the main means of providing public assistance towards solving the problems raised in this book.

LIMITATIONS OF EXISTING MEDIATION SERVICES

When any new development is suggested in this country one is invariably met with the reply: but we are doing it already and it hasn't solved the problem. These proposals for the expansion and development of constructive mediation services are likely to encounter this objection. The answer is framed largely in terms of the limitations and defects of existing services and in this connection two rather different points need to be made.

First, existing services are still affected by long-standing notions about their scope and objectives, which limit their impact and prevent them from developing in a sufficiently complementary way. Secondly, constructive mediation must be able to operate beyond the reach of day-to-day interventions in the interests of government policy. This can no longer be said of large parts of our existing public provisions in this field.

It is true that at first glance there are a wide variety of well established mediation services already in existence. These include the Department of Employment's Conciliation Service; its Manpower Advisory Service; its statutory powers to establish Courts of Inquiry, Committees of Investigation, Committees of Settlement, etc.; its provisions for arbitration, either through the Industrial Arbitration Board (formerly the Industrial Court) or through its panel of individual arbitrators and Boards of Arbitration. In addition there is the continuing work of the Commission on Industrial Relations and the Office of Manpower Economics.

But a multiplicity of agencies and forms of mediation cannot be taken as conclusive evidence of either comprehensiveness or adequacy. On further examination the services provided are far too limited and insufficiently co-ordinated. The roots of the limited objectives lie in the Conciliation Act of 1896. From the time of that Act the Department of Employment and its predecessors have been committed to operating a service, embodying two related principles – the preservation of 'voluntarism' and the maintenance of 'neutrality'. Our concern at the moment is with the limiting effects of the tradition of voluntarism. (The consequences of the doctrine of neutrality, and its gradual erosion, are discussed in the next section.)

In practice voluntarism has meant that conciliation officers have tried to avoid offering the parties direct advice as to how disputes should be settled. The aim of what might be termed 'classical' conciliation has been to 'clarify points of difference' in the hope that the parties would find their own way to an agreement. To take conciliation any further would be to encroach upon the area of voluntary action that has to be preserved for the parties themselves. More important, perhaps, is the fact that the doctrine of voluntarism has meant that until comparatively recently the skills and knowledge of conciliators were not available to deal with unofficial and unconstitutional disputes. For to interfere in situations where established procedure had not been fully exhausted was thought to undermine respect for that procedure, and was likely to reduce the authority and freedom of action of official negotiators.

Of course, as the number and impact of unofficial and unconstitutional strikes rose in the fifties and sixties this doctrine had to be relaxed to allow conciliation to be used to deal with the more obstinate and damaging of wildcat strikes. But it was still thought to be advisable to proceed with caution. Even today voluntarism means that involvement will not normally be suggested unless one of the parties requests the services of a conciliator. Moreover, mediation, in this form, is still viewed as a last resort. The aim of the Conciliation Service is still that of providing a minimum degree of third party assistance within a system that remains predominantly self-regulating. Consequently, although the case load of the Service has risen as the number and duration of disputes has increased, it is still an extremely small one in terms of most comparable systems. Moreover, on the last figures available the volume of activity has remained more or less stable for the last two years – i.e. Department of Employment conciliators have dealt with between 600 and 700 disputes a year.

Naturally the manner in which the Service has developed reflects the assumptions behind the notion of voluntarism. As we have seen these involve a belief in the adequacy and permanence of the formal system of industry-wide collective bargaining criticised by Donovan. The fact is that the Conciliation Service in this country was designed to cope with the exigencies of the formal system and still bears its imprint. It also continues to operate on a scale that assumes that there is nothing really wrong with that system. For this reason conciliation officers have, until quite recently, not been encouraged to direct the parties' attention to defects in their established bargaining arrangements. It is true that since the publication of the Donovan Report the situation has improved somewhat. Diagnostic and reformist techniques are now part of the conciliation officer's tool kit, and the Department of Employment is able to provide a professional and expert assessment of the adequacy or otherwise of a given procedural system. Yet the tendency still is to assume that the parties ought to be more or less convinced of the need for strategical mediation before it is even suggested to them, and one may legitimately doubt how far the Service can be expected to develop this side of its work in view of its growing involvement with the provisions of a controversial Industrial Relations Act.

Much the same reservations and doubts must be expressed about the future of other types of mediation – for example arbitration and inquiry. In fact arbitration has been even more restricted in its development, and in recent years use of the Department of Employment's provisions has declined. With the exception of two short wartime periods arbitration has never been systematically encouraged by the Department, for a variety of reasons. One factor relates to its alleged inflationary effects but almost as important, historically, has been the survival of the voluntarist assumption that too easy and frequent use of arbitration undermines the willingness of the parties to face up to their own responsibilities.

It is worth noting that this view continues to enjoy some support amongst trade unionists and managers – without, so far as we know, much validating evidence. Certainly it is not confirmed by the experiences of countries where third party dispute resolution is much more widely used than in Britain – for example Australia, North America and Scandinavia. There is also very little evidence that those industries in Britain which use arbitration as a more or less permanent feature of their own disputes procedures exhibit above average irresponsibility – for example, the Ball Clay industry, Cocoa, Chocolate and Sugar Confectionery, Civil Air Transport, Atomic Energy, Chemicals, Paint Varnish and Lacquer, Rubber Manufacture and so on. Moreover, there is no sign that plants or companies who have introduced arbitration into a new and more formal system of collective bargaining

have found that it has encouraged irresponsibility and a
reluctance to face up to problems on either side of the bargaining
table. On the contrary, the knowledge that arbitration is
available if the parties cannot agree often helps them to
continue their search for a compromise solution. This has
certainly been the case in American experience, where arbitration at the request of one party is the normal way of settling
most disputes arising during the period of an agreement.
Commenting on the situation in the US, Professor Jack
Stieber told the Donovan Commission that in 30% of its
cases the American National Academy of Arbitrators found
that no award was necessary because of subsequent 'withdrawals, settlements or cancellations'. Professor Stieber
concluded:

> 'This would seem to indicate that the availability of arbitra-
> tion does not necessarily stifle negotiations by the parties
> and may, in fact, tend to put pressure on the parties to reach
> their own decision rather than risk an arbitration award.'[2]

In the case of Courts of Inquiry and Committees of Investigation an additional problem has been that until very recently
they were largely viewed as extensions of the conciliation
process. Thus in many instances their terms of reference have
not allowed them to address themselves to anything one can
legitimately term strategical mediation. (Indeed, before the
creation of the Office of Manpower Economics it is doubtful
how far most governmental inquiry bodies were equipped to
investigate such problems in any depth.) To some extent the
existence of the OME, which has taken over some staff from the
former Prices and Incomes Board, offers a prospect of improvement, but once again the OME's terms of reference are
insufficiently wide and it is perhaps best equipped to examine
pay structures and pay principles in the public sector. As a
result the main burden for stimulating strategical mediation
in procedural matters, and in private industry generally, has
remained with the CIR. The CIR has made a useful contribution in this field in the past albeit on a somewhat limited
scale.

More recently its work has been dominated by the government's decision to use it as the main instrument for applying the detailed provisions of the 1971 Industrial Relations Act. Since most unions (and many employers) regard the Act as a partisan attempt to implement controversial government objectives in industrial relations – notably the aim of trade union bargaining restraint – this development has inevitably undermined the CIR's ability to operate as an 'independent' and acceptable instrument of strategical mediation.

But government partiality and partisanship has become an even more significant break on the development of independent and acceptable forms of tactical mediation for a somewhat longer period, and as a result of a rather different set of government objectives. It is necessary to trace this development more fully, partly in order to understand the mistaken premises on which it is based, but also in order to make clear what has to be avoided in future.

THE MOVE AWAY FROM NEUTRALITY

It was argued above that a too rigid adherence to the first principle of the 1896 Conciliation Act has acted as a restraining influence on the development of both kinds of mediation. The problem in respect of the second principle – the notion of neutrality – has been the exact reverse. It has been shown insufficient respect by successive governments over the last twenty years.

There can be no doubt that neutrality, or 'independence' remains one of the indispensable conditions of effective mediation in all its forms. Unless both sides believe that the mediator is, in some sense, impartial, they will not listen to his advice, or accept his judgement. (Indeed one or another of them will refuse to appear before him, or even ask for his services.) Yet it is important to stress that what independence means in practice is usually misunderstood – at least by those with no experience of mediation. The best mediators are not necessarily people without ideas of their own, who tamely accept the need to find 'safe' solutions to all problems. Resource-fulness and imagination are useful qualities in mediators, especially when they are combined with judgement and a keen sense of what is possible. Perception, curiosity and an ability to absorb new facts and developments are especially useful in the work of strategical mediation. But new ideas and approaches can also be useful in tactical mediation, especially when the parties are locked in a bitter and protracted dispute which has generated irritation and frustration on both sides. In situations like this it sometimes helps to have mediators who are prepared to suggest radical and untried solutions in the hope that they might form the basis for a settlement. Of course when mediation takes the form of a binding award or decision – which the parties undertake to accept in advance – mediators have to be more careful and circumspect. But even here it should not be assumed that there is no scope for imagination and judgement, so long as the mediator is seen to be observing the two golden rules of his trade. First, he must appear to have genuinely tried to search for a solution that is likely to be acceptable to both sides. Secondly, he must be seen to be indifferent to all forms of *external* manipulation or pressure. Today this usually means that he has to appear to be independent of government.

Until the mid-fifties both these principles were generally accepted by successive governments, but in recent years they have been increasingly undermined in practice. In the field of tactical mediation the main reason for this has been the search for a viable and effective incomes policy. This has meant that ministers have been casting around for effective levers to pull in order to exert some kind of influence on the pattern of immediate pay settlements. Unfortunately the public mediation service has appeared to them to be a fatally attractive and readily available lever.

Thus from time to time those who sit on public arbitration boards and committees have received letters from the govern-ment informing them of Ministers' views on the general level of settlements they ought to authorise. In other periods the Department of Employment's conciliators have been caught up in the task of implementing an increasingly unpopular and unrealistic incomes policy, and have sought to impose on the parties the criteria set out in successive government White Papers. (When they have failed the disputants have been warned that they were likely to be referred to a body such as the Prices and Incomes Board.) At other times, Governments have simply instructed the Conciliation Service to refuse to establish Committees of Investigation and Courts of Inquiry. Thus, recently the parties to a national dispute in local government were refused normal conciliation facilities by the Department of Employment in a letter which expressed the Government's arguments in an unusually frank and revealing way, and is worth quoting at some length:

'In the dispute between the two sides of the National Joint Council for Local Authorities' Manual Workers the employers have made an offer which would involve an increase in labour costs of the order of 14%. This is high by past and even present standards. A settlement at a higher figure would only add to the inflationary pressures from which all sections of the community – and in particular the lower paid workers – stand to lose.

'It would not be right for the conciliation services of the Department to be used to seek a settlement at a higher level and it is only fair to make clear in advance that if the Department were to respond to the request of the two sides for a further meeting, our efforts would have to be confined to trying to help the two sides to reach a settlement within the total amount already offered.'[3]

Needless to say this offer was refused. After a long and damaging strike the two sides had to establish their own form of mediation which helped to provide the basis for a settlement.

Policies of this kind would have to be openly and permanently repudiated if there is to be any hope of establishing support for the kind of extension of mediation services that we would like to see. This is stated without any desire to underestimate or ignore the influence of cost-induced inflation on Britain's social and economic difficulties in recent years, but rather to suggest that in this matter successive governments have employed inappropriate means. They have not appreciated that it is impossible to have any lasting effect on cost-induced inflation by the use of indirect pressure of this kind, and have failed to realise that they are essentially counter-productive, calculated to undermine confidence in mediation as such without *any* compensatory advantages.

The fight against inflation itself has been seriously hampered in the past by attempts to impose wage restraint by this back door method. First, because this policy naturally strikes workers as unfair and arbitrary, so that the very idea of an equitable and just 'incomes policy' is steadily destroyed. Second, because once blundered into, such policies have to be rationalised and justified by their authors. This means that it is difficult to direct their attention towards the real issues involved if attempts were to be made to develop really effective levers of influence.

Here, it seems to us, the beginning of wisdom lies in an acceptance of the fact that policies designed to influence income movements and incomes criteria must be separated from those policies designed to reform collective bargaining and contain industrial conflict; both in their day-to-day application and in their form of organisation. For the focus and emphasis of these policies is quite different, as are their purposes. The evidence for this statement is, perhaps, best demonstrated by reviewing, very briefly, the diversity of the elements that would need to be controlled if cost-push inflation were to be tackled seriously by any Government.

To begin with there are those factors that are not directly connected with income movements at all – e.g. patterns of government expenditure and taxation, methods of public and private finance, the structure and movement of interest rates, property prices and rent increases, etc. Then again, within the broad area of income movements there are both employment and non-employment factors – e.g. returns to property and share holdings and the income effects of capital accumulation. Moveover, even within employment income itself there are the factors that derive from individual as well as collective pay movements – i.e. managers who pay themselves an increase, or negotiate their increases face to face with the boss.

The trouble with trying to impose an incomes policy by denying conciliation and seeking to put pressure on arbitrators is that even if it were successful one would be only focusing on an extremely small element in the totality of factors involved – i.e. the two or three per cent of pay settlements that happen to be affected by mediation. And one could only expect even short-term success if there was reason to believe that such settlements were both disproportionately important and unusually high. But there is no evidence for either of these assertions.

In fact the majority of pay disputes where mediation is involved are comparatively small in scale – i.e. those involving the day-to-day activities of the Department of Employment's regional Conciliation Service. It is true that from time to time Courts of Inquiry and Boards of Arbitration are employed to help solve a few of the more important national disputes – such as those that have occurred recently in local government, electricity supply and the coal industry; but even here there is little if any evidence that mediation, as such, has added significantly to the forces of cost-induced inflation.

The fact that newspapers like the *Economist* continue to thunder to the contrary only demonstrates their ignorance of the nature of the bargaining process. They have not heard of the 'without prejudice' offer. They do not know that in most disputes of this kind a 'private' offer has usually been made to the unions by the employers 'without prejudice' to the position that the latter intend to adopt if they are forced to defend their case in public. Not unnaturally this offer is usually significantly above that made public at the time, and the unions have to take the chance that they can convince a Court of Inquiry, or an arbitrator, that they deserve more than this. Unfortunately the public, many journalists and even ministers, who should know better, only appear to know about the 'public' offer. Consequently the mediator's decision, when it is known, is often denounced as unduly high.

A well-known recent example of this reaction was, of course, the award of the Scamp Tribunal, which was set up privately by the two sides to deal with the local government workers' claim after normal conciliation by the Department of Employment had been refused. Sir Jack Scamp and his colleagues were able to secure a rapid return to work in this dispute, thus bringing an end to an extremely disruptive and costly strike. But their award, when it was made public, was denounced in the Press, on television and in the House of Commons. They were said to be arch feeders of the fires of inflation. What was not so widely publicised was that the Scamp award was only a fraction above the private offer made to the unions in negotiation. Without Scamp it is undeniable that the strike in local government would have lingered on for several more weeks; but what is highly questionable is that the settlement, when it came, would have been any lower.

Since the Scamp Award similar judgements have been passed by commentators in other dispute situations – most notably the electricity go-slow and the miners' strike in 1972. In both these cases mediation, in the form of an acceptable Court of Inquiry, was eventually agreed after a long and disruptive dispute. The results were denounced as inflationary, but it was very difficult to believe that without the help of mediation the parties themselves would have managed to agree on a lower settlement. What did seem reasonably clear was that it might have taken them longer. What was suggested was that an earlier use of mediation, in a more readily acceptable form, could have saved the public a great deal of inconvenience.

The truth is that given the consensual and voluntary nature of mediation, by and large the level and form taken by the small minority of pay settlements that have been subjected to the mediation process is bound to reflect, rather than lead, the standard set by the great majority of settlements that are the result of direct negotiations. So far as we know this is the case in all forms and systems of mediation so far invented. Moreover, in the case of Britain this has been demonstrated in respect of the most sustained and influential form of arbitration so far experienced – i.e. the work of the Industrial Disputes Tribunal.[4]

The IDT operated a form of legally binding arbitration in Britain from 1951 to 1959. It was the relic of more far-reaching war-time legislation which was continued into the post-war period, largely because it was thought to assist in preventing disruptive strike action in vital parts of the public sector. One of the rules of the Tribunal was that it would consider cases brought at the request of only one party. Partly as a result of this it had a considerable case load and in the eight years of its life the IDT made over 1,270 awards. All kinds and types of employers and unions appeared before the IDT – including many powerful groups such as the boilermakers, the sheet metal workers, the printers and the dockworkers. If arbitration was a significant independent cause of cost-induced inflation one would expect to see some evidence of this in IDT decisions.

Certainly many people thought that this was the case at the time, and it is now generally admitted that the then Minister of Labour, Iain Macleod, took the decision to press for the abolition of the IDT primarily because *he* thought its awards were inflationary. In fact there is absolutely no evidence for this belief, and what evidence there is points in the reverse direction. In his study of IDT awards, which formed the basis for the Donovan Commission's inquiries, Moshe Reiss con-concluded that in the great majority of cases, IDT decisions appeared to reflect what 'appeared to be the "going rate" '. Indeed after comparing IDT awards with known pay increases granted by other methods over the whole period of its existence the Donovan Commission's summary of Reiss's findings concludes:

> 'Granted the imperfect nature of these figures they do show a considerable degree of similarity. If anything the IDT awards are generally slightly below those arrived at by other methods – but the difference is not substantial.'[5]

Unfortunately the Commision failed to draw the obvious conclusions from Reiss's work. It actually fed the misapprehensions of those who have continued to regard mediation as a prime cause of cost-induced inflation by recommending 'legislation placing on all arbitrators an obligation to take incomes policy into account when making their awards'.[6] It should be clear by now that it is because we wish to see a realistic attempt to tackle inflation that we favour a more comprehensive and less partisan approach. This book is not about inflation, or even its cost push elements, so that this is not the place to discuss the subject in detail. What is clear, however, is that any policy, if it is to be successful in the long term, must aim to deal with *all* the factors affecting rising prices in a more or less equitable way. There must be no special penalties lying in wait for those who opt for mediation rather than resort to strike action; just as there should be no special focus on public sector pay settlements.

Personally we would favour an approach in the bargaining field similar to that outlined by Clegg in his recent study *How to run an Incomes Policy and why we made such a mess of the last one.*[7] We support his suggestion that pay criteria should be linked to movements in the cost of living, and that there should be exceptions for special cases. Our principal disagreement with Clegg is about how he sees the role of the law in the direct enforcement of wage restraint and the insignificance he attaches to the legal regulation of prices. In our view it would be preferable to link such legal regulation as is required to the control of factors affecting price movements, although we appreciate that where wages can be shown to be a cause of unjustified price rises they will have to be tackled as well.

Given this approach it seems that the government's recent introduction of a statutorily based policy is unlikely to provide a long term solution to the problem of inflation. It is true that during 'phase two' an attempt will be made to tackle some of the non-wage elements of cost-induced inflation, but this is being done on a less than comprehensive basis – for example in respect of capital gains. And nothing is promised yet to deal with 'special cases' before 'phase three' begins, while the pay norm in the policy is unrelated to movements in the cost of living. Certainly there is a form of price control in operation, but this is without any direct link between price control and wage restraint. Yet great reliance is placed upon the legal control of wages, without any support from the trade unions.

Most important of all, from the standpoint of this book, although the Pay Board has power to review negotiated settlements as well as awards reached through arbitration, there is no guarantee that attempts will not be made to exercise a disproportionate influence upon mediators by the usual 'back door' methods. It is not yet appreciated that if an incomes policy is acceptable to trade unions and employers it will be reflected in the kinds of claims they make, or in the level of settlements that they are prepared to accept. And even if this is not the case, while the policy is not so rigid as to rule out all forms of adjustment and movement in wages, attempts to buttress it by the law should be done in ways that do not put a premium on strikes. In practice this means that any legal sanctions which are employed are best imposed after the mediator has completed his task. Any other policy is designed to destroy what respect there remains for all forms of mediation; on wage and other issues.

Fortunately there are some signs that the dangers of seeking to nobble mediators, in the so-called interests of price stability, are at last being recognised outside government circles. One indication of this was the creation of an 'independent' or 'neutral' mediation panel by the CBI and the TUC. It is known that there are forces within this body who want it to develop to the point where it largely supercedes the mediation functions of the Department of Employment. These ideas are similar to those we develop further in the section below.

THE ORGANISATION OF MEDIATION SERVICES

It is assumed from this point that the case for constructive mediation has been established. It is also assumed that the limitations of existing provisions have been demonstrated, and that fears that expansion of such services might encourage irresponsibility and/or inflation can now be disregarded. The rest of the chapter is therefore concerned with outlining how these services might be organised in order that they are effectively used. A number of examples are given of how they might be expected to work in practice.

As we see it their organisational structure should be designed to promote four main objectives:

1 The maximum involvement of serving trade unionists and practising managers in the overall administration of the service;
2 The development of a full-time staff of mediation officers, based on local communities and serving their needs;
3 A policy of developing the work load of the services through industrial contacts, especially at shop floor level;
4 The encouragement of inter-related types of services, designed to stress the connection between tactical and strategical mediation.

One of the main advantages to be gained from adopting the first principle is that it provides the best means of guaranteeing the services continued independence of government. Another is that it helps to ensure that mediators will respond to the actual needs of the parties, and this should assist in making mediation more acceptable in their eyes. Many serving trade unionists and practising managers can assist the process of mediation, and may make good mediators themselves. Above all their practical experience of industry and its problems should be drawn on wherever possible. Since mediation facilities are needed at regional or local level we wish to see a service where the day-to-day running of much of the work would be under the overall supervision of part-time lay committees, operating within a budget determined centrally. Serving on such area mediation committees would be a variety of suitably qualified people, but the majority would be drawn from the local industrial community. Most importantly, leading shop stewards and practising personnel managers would be encouraged to be actively involved.

Area mediation committees would have at their disposal a full-time staff, which, in the first instance, would have to be drawn from the Department of Employment's Conciliation Service and its manpower advisers. But this source would need to be rapidly supplemented by others drawn from outside the Civil Service. Fortunately the experience of recent expansions of conciliation and manpower advisory work and the recruitment of suitable staff for bodies like the Prices and Incomes Board and the CIR, indicates that there are no real problems here in respect of management personnel. The problems that do exist mainly concern trade union representatives. Unions understandably find it difficult to release full-time officers to work for institutions of this kind on a temporary basis, and by and large the best type of trade union official is often reluctant to sever his connections with the trade union movement permanently. Our solution would be a series of specially designed short-term secondments, tailor-made to fit in with the promotion of union officers and their movement from job to job. Furthermore, every effort would need to be made to see that the union concerned was fully compensated when releasing officials to do this kind of work.

The most important section of the locally based staff would be the group of mediation officers working 'in the field'. They would be expected to establish and maintain contacts with firms and unions throughout their area. In effect they would be the ambassadors of the new service, and it would be part of their job to spread knowledge and information about the full range of facilities available. They would be expected to be rather more positive and innovative in stimulating a demand for mediation than is the case in respect of the existing regional staff of the Department of Employment. For they would be committed to promoting the widest possible use of local and national facilities – although the presence of lay committees would ensure that this was done with tact and discretion.

So much for the first two principles whose advantages would appear to be self evident. The case for the third is, perhaps, in need of rather more explanation. It seems to us that in the recent past too much mediation has appeared to arise in ways insufficiently related to the felt needs of the parties involved. This was, perhaps, most obviously the case in respect of the work of the late Prices and Incomes Board. The Board was responsible for some of the most far-sighted proposals for bargaining reform yet seen in this country – and on many occasions its suggestions led to considerable improvements being introduced in bargaining structures. It is true that its work in the field of strategical mediation was sometimes affected, and made more difficult, by the Board's involvement with the implementation of incomes policy, but this was not the only problem. Part of the trouble arose because the Board received its work-load directly from the government, in the form of a series of specific 'references'. Moreover, the Board itself, from its inception, emphasised its own right to conduct its own investigations, and to reach its own conclusions. Those affected by its reports were not allowed to see them before they were published, and were not even supposed to be informed of the kind of proposals the Board intended to make before they were made available to the Press. There is considerable evidence that this style of operation did not help to make the Board more acceptable to either side of industry, and sometimes it resulted in serious errors and miscalculations that could have been avoided if the Board's relationships with the parties had been more continuous and close.

To some extent, in the first period of its operations the CIR sought to learn from these deficiencies. Yet the CIR was itself subjected to a rather bizarre procedure for the selection of its references. This involved a certain amount of 'top level' consultation with representatives of the CBI and TUC. But few who have experienced this process would claim that it was close to the shop floor. As a result those most affected by references in individual companies and plants usually thought that they had been chosen on somewhat dubious grounds, largely in order to provide the CIR with what was termed 'a balanced programme of work'.

At the same time tactical mediation was being increasingly affected by the results of the move away from neutrality referred to earlier in this chapter. The result was that in this area too the parties came to feel that their needs and requirements were not being taken into account.

Consequently a legacy of suspicion has developed which will need to be rapidly overcome if the aims set out earlier in the chapter are to be realised. And linking the mediation case load more formally and openly with the industrial needs of the parties – especially as they are manifested at local level – seems to us to be one of the best ways of accomplishing this objective. Thus we would not expect much of the work of these reformed and expanded mediation services to originate in the form of government 'references'. The area mediation committees, together with the national mediation board, established to co-ordinate their activities, would by and large determine their own work load. And in the case of the areas the day-to-day work of the field officers would provide the bulk of references.

This is not to say that the government would be excluded from all forms of influence. It would have to be responsible for providing the annual budget for all mediation services, and would have formal responsibility for appointing members of the national mediation board. It also seems only reasonable to give the government the right to instruct the board to undertake important and far-reaching investigations on its behalf. The government would also retain the right to establish additional *ad hoc* inquiries of its own, under the terms of the existing conciliation Acts. But it would be generally understood that for the bulk of their work, the new mediation services would be expected to look outwards and downwards, rather than inwards and upwards. Ultimate public control could be assured by means of an annual report to Parliament by the members of the national board.

The arguments for encouraging inter-related mediation activities are best developed in the final section of this chapter, which aims to provide a number of practical examples of how these new services might help to improve industrial relations. It will suffice to say at the moment that it is our opinion that it is almost always the case that successful mediation of one kind helps to open up the way for equally useful mediation of a different kind. One of the criticisms we would make of existing mediation services is that they do not encourage a mutually beneficial interchange between tactical and strategical mediation. But perhaps it is time to give some examples of how constructive mediation might operate in practice.

HOW CONSTRUCTIVE MEDIATION COULD HELP

We begin with two examples from private industry, where the focus would be on assisting the parties in dealing with plant or company problems of the kind discussed by Donovan. We may suppose that the first arises where a management is involved in a recognition dispute – say with one or more white collar unions. At the moment a situation of this kind is a natural subject for conciliation by a Department of Employment conciliation officer. What we are suggesting is that in future when conciliation is successful in promoting a settlement it should be regarded as natural and normal for the officer concerned to stress the need to develop an adequate framework of jointly agreed rules to deal with the likely consequences of recognising trade unions. Thus the inevitable implications of union recognition on established salary structures and the role of supervisors would need to be emphasised together with the need for adequate shop steward facilities and training. As a result the area mediation committee might be asked to sponsor a diagnostic survey to be conducted by a member of its staff. Members of the committee would be available to discuss the results of this exercise with the parties involved. This could lead to further collective agreements being negotiated covering many of the matters raised in the report. These might well involve the use of mediation to deal with certain kinds of future disputes on a more systematic basis – say by the use of independent arbitration. Arbitrators would be drawn from a panel compiled by members of the area committee. (Indeed, where possible, members of the committee would be encouraged to undertake some of this work themselves.)

Our second example concerns a more difficult situation where a local field officer becomes aware that a plant or firm has a rising record of strikes. So far none of these has resulted in a request for mediation, but within the system we propose that would not be thought to prevent an initiative by the local officer. He could initiate a discussion between both sides of general industrial relations problems, as a result of which it might be agreed that the roots of many disputes lay in a defective payments system and its impact on a well established, but now largely unobserved, disputes procedure.

At this point the local mediation officer might propose a review of alternative payment systems and their procedural implications, to be carried out with the assistance of specialist staff from the national mediation board. But if the report of a working party established to find a new pay structure failed to provide a basis for agreement, then the mediation officer would withdraw to observe events. In time relationships might improve, partly as a result of the discussion of joint problems touched off by the activities of the working party. This could in time lead to joint agreement on a programme of bargaining reform, although the details might not resemble the proposals first advanced in the original review of alternative pay systems and procedures.

Alternatively, relationships might continue to deteriorate and the level of strikes increase. Eventually a prolonged and difficult dispute could arise, in the course of which mediation was used to promote a settlement. The climate might then make possible a new initiative; perhaps a more far-reaching general inquiry into the causes of industrial unrest, conducted by an area-based committee of investigation under the chairmanship of one of the members of the local area committee. Part of their report could suggest an extension of spheres of joint decision-taking, including moves in the direction of predictive bargaining. On the assumption that the parties agreed to implement bargaining reforms based on such a report, local and national mediation services might be required to assist in providing advice on management and shop steward training.

Our third example of local action is drawn from the public sector. There is considerable scope for both strategical and tactical mediation in this field – though it was largely ignored by the Donovan Commission. Here we may suppose that as the result of a national wage settlement in the Health Service a change in wage structures has been linked to the introduction of performance targets. Mediation services, at national level, agree to participate in a procedure for jointly monitoring the implementation of the agreement at local level. As a result it becomes apparent that in many areas management and staff side representatives are ill-equipped to deal with some of the problems and on management side there is a lack of expertise in techniques of job appraisal. In this situation there is clearly scope for local action by mediation officers. They should be able to offer individual hospital authorities the necessary assistance and advice. If necessary their experience could be pooled by the national board to sponsor a new approach to the problem, which could take the form of a report into the whole field of management structure and practice. This could lead to a realisation that many problems in the Health Service are rooted in an inadequate system of joint decision-taking, and the retention of outdated notions of managerial prerogatives. If so, proposals would be advanced for extending the range and subject matter of collective bargaining, at national and local level.

So far the examples chosen have largely concentrated on the kind of mediation work that would be sponsored or undertaken by area mediation committees. Chapter Four showed that the Donovan Commission over-emphasised in certain respects the industrial relations problems of individual plants and companies and partly for this reason it tended to overlook, or disregard, the need for reform beyond the level of the individual enterprise. One of the main functions of the national mediation board could be to encourage and sponsor this kind of work. This chapter therefore concludes with three examples of how it might operate in this field.

Our first example is taken from the docks. At first glance it might appear as if this industry has already been the subject of a surfeit of mediation – since the time of Ernie Bevin's first appearance as the Dockers' QC before the 1920 Court of Inquiry. But although it is true that there have been many public inquiries on the docks, they have been spasmodic in their incidence and unduly limited in their terms of reference, and have not been followed by adequate monitoring procedures. Thus the history of mediation in the docks serves as another illustration of the limitations and defects of the existing range of public services that we wish to remedy.

To make this point effectively it is not necessary to go beyond the report of the Devlin Committee in 1965. Devlin found that the partial decasualisation scheme advocated by Bevin in 1919, and finally implemented in 1946, had not fulfilled expectations. Partly because of the proliferation of small employers, and the growth of inequitable piecework systems, job security and earnings stability had not been achieved. Largely as a result of this all kinds of restrictive labour practices had developed making the British docks a by-word for inefficiency. To solve these problems Devlin suggested the elimination of the small employer, complete decasualisation and the abolition of the piecework system. To help gain agreement for more efficient working methods a system of electing shop stewards was also proposed.

There can be little doubt that given the situation they inherited in 1964, and their own narrow terms of reference, the Devlin Committee's recommendations were sensible and practical. The trouble was that the Committee failed to anticipate several new developments that have arisen since 1965. Those have combined to destroy most of the benefits that should have accrued from the implementation of its Report. The most important of these developments was, of course, the decline in the demand for traditional dock work which has resulted from the rapid growth of inland containerisation. Another factor has been the introduction of 'non-registered' dock labour to undertake the 'stuffing and stripping' of containers in dockland areas. Also of considerable significance has been the movement of dock work to the smaller ports.

By the beginning of 1972 these developments had produced a serious decline in the take-home pay of many dockers, fears of large-scale redundancy and a legacy of growing bitterness and militancy. The inevitable result was widespread unofficial action, which in the context of the 1971 Industrial Relations Act brought the dockers leaders and their union into conflict with the law. Eventually, after a prolonged and extremely damaging national strike, the report of yet another committee (Jones-Aldington) suggested a further programme of bargaining reform.

Our main point is simply that the existence of the kind of national mediation board we would like to see could have prevented many of these developments. To begin with, the 1944 scheme would not have been allowed to deteriorate for so long before suggestions were made for its improvement. And even if reform had been delayed for more than twenty years, the Committee established to consider the problems of the docks would have been given much wider terms of reference. This might well have been asked to look at the case for extending the scope of the National Dock Labour Scheme to include the smaller ports, and would certainly have been asked to prepare a detailed manpower forecast.

Most important of all, in the case of a major industry such as the docks, it would be normal for the national mediation board to be given some responsibility for monitoring the results of any proposals for reform. In this way the employment effects of containerisation, or the introduction of non-traditional labour, would have been detected long before the consequences of doing nothing about them had become so explosive. In a word, under the system proposed here, it would not have been necessary to imprison workers, fine their union and endure a national dock strike, before embarking on a further attempt to get to the roots of the problem.

On the contrary, one of the main aims of constructive mediation is to maintain a watching brief in situations of this kind. And where the problem is an industry-wide one we would expect the national mediation board to take action designed to promote reform before the position had deteriorated to the near chaos of the docks at the time of Jones-Aldington. To help make this point we have chosen our two remaining examples from industries where the signs of existing strain are, as yet, less apparent. We shall describe the industrial relations problems of these industries more briefly, but enough will be said to indicate that both provide opportunities for action by a national mediation board.

Our first example is construction. In this industry the crucial difficulty is that the established system of industry-wide collective bargaining has failed to cope with the consequences of an unstable labour market and low levels of supervision. As a result more and more employers have developed their own systems of site bonuses, and these have usually been extremely crude and inequitable. It is true that these systems have enabled some workers to earn very high wages for short periods, but at the cost of a rapid decline in work standards and a deterioration in the supply of skilled labour to the industry. For some years now the larger and more responsible contractors have tried to reverse this process – by developing site and company agreements based on systems of work measurement. But their efforts are constantly undermined by the inability of the mass of small firms to follow their example – especially where they are committed to a policy of 'labour only' subcontracting.

In September 1972 the inequities and uncertainties that resulted from this situation erupted in the form of a national building strike. The militancy and determination shown by many workers in the course of that dispute, and their relative dissatisfaction with its outcome, are an indication that the industry will face continuing industrial unrest unless and until something is done at national level to provide a more effective framework of joint-regulation.

It should be obvious that we have no simple solutions to advance for the difficulties of the building industry, and if we had this would not be the place to discuss them. Our point is merely that here is another example of an industry where constructive mediation at national level could help. First, because the parties themselves lack the resources to undertake the studies required. Second, because some of the solutions may require initiatives to be taken in co-operation with government (for example, the development of an overall manpower plan for the industry, or measures of 'decasualisation' involving the registration of qualified workers and contractors.) It would seem that proposals of this kind are best evaluated and advanced by an independent body like the national mediation board, which can pronounce more objectively on their consequences and benefits in terms of the national economy.

For our final example we turn to the public sector and consider the position of local government. Here there is a rather different set of problems. First, there is the fact that both wage and salary earners are supposed to be governed by a highly centralised form of collective bargaining based on the National Joint Council for Local Authority Services in Belgrave Square, London. The NJC agrees a structure of standard rates of pay which is intended to apply without variation over the entire country. In fact local councils find that they have to find ways of varying the application of these rates to take into account their own circumstances, including the state of the local labour market. Thus councils in high employment and high cost areas have introduced bogus bonus schemes for manual workers and have manipulated salary scales to pay white collar workers in short supply more money when required. This has led to increasing dissatisfaction and a growing sense of inequity amongst groups excluded from this process, especially when the local authority concerned has introduced unworkable schemes that have failed to result in the level of earnings promised by the management.

Problems of this sort have also not been helped by the period of uncertainty and change that has existed in local government for several years – largely as a result of a series of government plans for introducing far-reaching changes in the boundaries of local authorities and their relative functions. Then there is the fact that the traditional reliance on the national machinery at Belgrave Square has meant that many councils have been encouraged to adopt a relatively disinterested attitude towards their own responsibilities as employers. Finally, and in some ways most damaging of all, there is the dilemma which faces all local authorities as a result of the way in which local government is financed in this country – i.e. through an increasingly inequitable and unsatisfactory system of local rate levies. This system has the effect of making local councillors regard all demands for an improvement in wages or working conditions as a threat to existing rate levels. (And there is a traditional belief among local councillors that he who agrees to a rise in rates undermines his electoral support.)

Solutions to any of these problems are not offered in this book; our point is that once again they could form the basis for a useful exercise in strategical mediation undertaken by the national mediation board. First, because there would seem to be a need for an objective and detached study of the policy implications of seeking to move towards, say, a more flexible wage and salary structure through national negotiations. Second, because once again issues are involved that would require action to be taken at national level, possibly by Government – e.g. a modification or reform of the system of financing local government services by a system of rate levies.

We also have no wish to try to spell out here how the national board might become involved in the problems of these industries. It could be via a form of tactical mediation – i.e. their use as a conciliator or arbitrator in a national dispute. On the other hand it might be that they would first be called in by unions and employers in one of the larger companies and authorities; where their ability to help would lead to an invitation at national level. Or it could be that in either or both of these industries the request for the services of the board would be initiated by one or more of the unions. In local government there are examples of this in the past. In the construction industry it is well known that some union leaders wanted the last building dispute to end in an agreement to conduct a joint investigation of wage structure problems, with the help of the new TUC–CBI conciliation and arbitration service.

Of course investigations of this kind would not make up the whole of the work of the national board. It would be needed to provide all kinds of support to area committees, and sometimes difficult and complicated cases arising at local level might be passed upwards to the board. It would also operate its own tactical mediation services to deal with important industry-wide disputes. Finally, the board would have a responsibility for drawing up a series of industrial relations principles capable of being embodied in model agreements. Examples of the principles it might favour include: the separation of disputes arising over their application (i.e. the so-called distinction between disputes of 'right' and disputes of 'interest'); the promotion of arbitration provisions in collective agreements, especially on rights issues; procedures for the reduction and elimination of multi-unionism; techniques for reviewing the adequacy of procedures and payment systems. In general the board would be expected to promote the extension of systems of joint regulation and would be specifically concerned to explore and develop practical examples of new methods of achieving this objective – e.g. by the negotiation of systems of predictive bargaining.

THE ARGUMENT SO FAR

We have now completed most of our answers to the issues posed at the end of chapter Five. The nature of the shop floor challenge discussed by the Donovan Commission and others has been re-examined, and linked to the other major challenge now facing British management. A new approach aimed at facilitating an adjustment between these two challenges has been described – based on an extension and transformation of conventional collective bargaining. This chapter has mainly been concerned with devising and describing institutions to help this process along, by means of various forms of mediation.

To make the case for an extended use of mediation in a more positive and comprehensive form, it was necessary to analyse the defects and drawbacks of our existing mediation services. We concluded that they were too limited in their objectives and facilities and, in recent years, insufficiently independent in their mode of operation. The organisational structure we proposed to take their place was designed to promote a much closer involvement by serving trade unionists and practising managers at all levels of its operation. It was also suggested that the new services should normally be expected to generate most of their own case load, and that they should operate in such a way that there was a close inter-action between different types and different levels of mediation.

It should now be clear why the term constructive mediation has been employed to describe this range of services. As we see it, the services would have as one of their main objectives the promotion of systems of joint-regulation as a means of providing for the adjustment and resolution of all forms of industrial conflicts. In this sense their work will be informed by a consistent and constructive search after methods of promoting industrial democracy and industrial peace.

To further their work the national and area committees charged with these tasks would be expected to launch initiatives and to make suggestions to both sides. Yet they will have to remember that mediation, in the final analysis, has to be felt to be required by the parties themselves. We are not proposing the creation of an expensive network of public institutions, whose main aim will be to pester practical men of affairs in an effort to drum up business. It would have to be content with the task of creating facilities and publicising them. The fact that they will be meeting a long-felt gap in our existing system of industrial relations, will be sufficient in our view to guarantee an adequate flow of cases. Certainly we are not thinking of *compulsory* mediation in any form. We believe this to be a contradiction in terms.

However, there will be a need for an appropriate legal framework to underpin and promote both the aims of management by agreement and the extension of all forms of constructive mediation. These matters are the subject of the chapter which follows.

Notes

1 Clark Kerr, *Labour and Management in Industrial Society*, Doubleday, 1964, p. 180.
2 Donovan Report, Research paper 8: *Grievance Arbitration in the United States: an Analysis of its Functions and Effects*, by Jack Stieber, HMSO, 1968, p. 7.
3 *Incomes Data Services* Number 35, August, 1972.
4 Donovan Report, Research Paper 8, *Compulsory Arbitration in Britain: The Work of the Industrial Disputes Tribunal*, by W. E. J. McCarthy, HMSO, 1968.
5 Ibid., p. 39.
6 Donovan Report, p. 72.
7 H. A. Clegg, *How to run an Incomes Policy and why we made such a mess of the last one*, Heinemann, 1971.

8. What the law can do

'My first duty in giving these Hamlyn Lectures is to put my cards on the table and make a confession . . . the law can only make a modest contribution to the people's standard of life.'

'What the lawyer can do and what the legislator can do remains important, far more important is the work of the engineer and scientist, the practical economist and the creative organiser. My second confession, then, is one of humility. I regard law as a secondary force in human affairs, and especially in labour relations.'

OTTO KAHN-FREUND[1]

One of the main arguments of this book has been that the 1971 Industrial Relations Act fails to recognise the legitimate and effective limits of legal regulation in industrial relations. It is at once too ambitious and too all-embracing. It aims to restrain and tame the over-mighty power of 'irresponsible trade unionism', while at the same time furthering the cause of bargaining reform. Enough has been said about why we think that the first of these objectives is mistaken and incompatible with the second. An alternative policy has been presented and the kind of institutions which would be needed to stimulate and promote it. This chapter suggests an appropriate legal framework to assist in the attainment of these objectives.

While agreeing with Professor Kahn-Freund that the law is a 'secondary force' in labour relations we consider that it can help the process of reform in a number of ways. We shall be searching for legal rules which serve to encourage moves in the direction of 'management by agreement' and the use of constructive mediation. This chapter seeks to answer the question: given that everything has been done to encourage reform by voluntary means, what else can be accomplished with the aid of the law?

In our view an appropriate legal framework would promote six principle objectives:

1 The development of representative negotiators on both sides of the bargaining table, able and willing to enter into agreements leading to a greater degree of joint control over decisions taken in their firm or industry, and able to persuade those they represent to co-operate in their implementation and observance.

2 A network of independent mediation services, exercising an increasing influence on the process of bargaining reform and the resolution of industrial disputes.

3 A comprehensive and balanced range of lawful industrial sanctions, available to both sides when there is a failure to agree.

4 A framework of individual rights for workers *vis-à-vis* trade unions and management.

5 Laws to promote more effective trade union services and the development of union resources.

6 A way of formulating legal rights and obligations that is comprehensible at the workplace on both sides of industry.

THE DEVELOPMENT OF REPRESENTATIVE NEGOTIATORS

On the workers' side two crucial forms of legal support for trade union organisation are required. These may be termed the *right to combine* and the *right to representation*.

The Right to Combine

The law can help in this area if framed along the lines suggested by the Donovan Commission. Its proposal making it illegal to dismiss or discriminate on grounds of membership or participation in an independent organisation of workers should be implemented. But there is no justification in restricting this right to membership or activity in a registered union – along the lines of the present Act. As was said in chapter Four the Act confuses the purposes of registration. Registration should be seen as a device for regulating the internal rules of voluntary associations; a way of seeking to ensure that they observe certain standards in respect of their members. There are in fact more acceptable ways of dealing with these matters; but even if this were not the case there would be no justification for legislating to create a situation where the worker who wishes to join a union which is not registered has no protection if his employer decides to sack him. As was argued above, the authors of the Act found themselves committed to this indefensible cause largely because they wished to provide unions with an incentive to register. In the event they have proved largely unsuccessful; meanwhile the results are unfair in respect of the great majority of union members.

Otherwise the provisions of the Act relating to the right to combine seem reasonable enough, though there may be a cas e for spelling out in more detail what is meant by the right o participate in union activities (i.e. it should involve the right to minimum facilities for contacting members). There is also need for a more precise definition of what is to count as an 'independent' union, but we return to this matter below.

The Right to Representation

Again we would favour following the method suggested by the Donovan Commission, although here our desire to advance the cause of management by agreement by the extension of systems of joint-regulation favours a more adventurous approach. Donovan proposed that any independent union with members in a firm should be able to apply to the CIR for an investigation of their 'right to be recognised'. If the Commission thought them appropriate and representative of a significant number of workers involved, it would normally be expected to recommend recognition and the right to bargain.

The 1971 Act followed Donovan's proposals in its broad outline, but it included several important modifications which we have argued are undesirable. First, the right to take cases to the CIR is once again unjustifiably and illogically confined to registered unions. Second, established systems of recognition and representation are put at risk by what we have termed the Act's 'revocation procedures'. Third, once a union, employer, or dissident work group invokes the intervention of the CIR, action to obtain recognition in other ways becomes actionable. There is no case for retaining any of these provisions, but the Donovan proposals should be modified in two other respects.

First, recognition is an 'open-ended' affair and the legislation should embody this fact. That is to say, a claim for recognition means very different things in different circumstances; ranging from the position where the employer simply agrees to meet with union representatives, but will not enter into collective agreements on their behalf, through to the situation where a union is already accepted as having a right to bargain over a broad range of subjects but management is still refusing to recognise it for certain additional purposes. What has to be appreciated is that even unions who have been accorded a measure of recognition can find themselves involved in a recognition dispute; for this can arise at any point along the continuum. In this situation a claim for recognition amounts to an assertion, on the union's part, that its desire to push forward the frontier of joint control is being resisted by management. Unfortunately the Donovan Commission wrote as if recognition was simply a once for all issue. Consequently, its proposals for dealing with this problem are mechanistic and rather crude.

To remedy this defect it should be made clear that any union can register a recognition dispute with the appropriate mediation service covering any subject or aspect of management decision-taking. For example, a union may allege that an employer has refused to grant adequate shop steward facilities, or to discuss manning levels, disciplinary and dismissal questions, or promotion.

In deciding whether or not the union has a case for increased recognition the appropriate division of the National Mediation Board would have to take into account a wide range of factors, including the willingness of the union to become involved in meaningful attempts to secure agreement on ways of tackling the external problems facing the firm – for example, through the medium of predictive bargaining. It would not be the intention to give legal support to claims for recognition in this advanced form in a random or arbitrary way. Nevertheless, the declared aim should be to assist in moving forward the frontiers of joint decision-taking wherever and whenever appropriate. The intention should be to encourage the growth of more sophisticated bargaining systems and a movement in the direction of management by agreement. Managers who refused to grant a union further recognition in this sense would be subject to similar sanctions to those facing a demand for what one might term 'primary recognition' – that is to say they would be liable to find themselves in front of an independent arbitration tribunal, where the union would be arguing its case for some degree of joint control in an area of management decision-taking which had previously been within the 'sacred garden' of managerial prerogatives. Naturally they would want to appear before such a tribunal to explain their case against the proposed changes. In effect the joint regulation of this area would have begun.

The same procedure could be used to deal with the problem of employers who refuse to disclose relevant information to trade unionists in the course of collective bargaining. The 1971 Act tries to deal with this problem along the lines of the last Labour Government's draft Bill on the subject. Consequently it raises all kinds of complex and often unnecessary questions about the kind of information that should be made generally available to trade unions. It has also made it possible for employers to refuse to disclose such information on a wide variety of grounds – i.e. that it may prejudice their trading position, or national security and so on. There seems to be no reason to raise many of these problems or difficulties, if the right to information is firmly embodied in the procedure outlined above.

A union able to show that it could not consider its reaction to a management demand, or formulate a relevant claim of its own, because of a lack of information, could complain to the appropriate division of the mediation service. In general the firm in question would be legally bound to disclose the required information to officers of the service, who would decide whether there was a case for releasing it to the union. In cases where the firm had established the need to maintain confidentiality the union would be given access to a form of independent arbitration where the information would be available to the arbitrator on a confidential basis. In this way it would still be possible to take it into account in arriving at a settlement.

The other way in which the Donovan proposals could be modified and extended relates to the need to promote the reduction of multi-unionism. It has already been said that in this respect the revocation provisions of the Act do not help, but in other ways the Act does try to deal with this problem. It sets out criteria for evaluating the appropriateness of bargaining units and their agents that are for the most part reasonable. The main criticism of them is that they fail to give the investigating body sufficient guidance, and most important, they contain no direct injunction to seek to prevent and restrain the forces of fractionalisation in trade union representation. They could be equally compatible with the encouragement and promotion of breakaway organisations, even if the revocation procedures themselves were rescinded.

This defect should be remedied by stipulating that when considering the appropriateness of bargaining agents in recognition cases the mediation service ought to place a special emphasis on discouraging new and factionalist organisations where appropriate trade unions already exist. Those considering claims for recognition should be instructed to actively promote the elimination of multi-union channels of communication – say through the promotion of the Donovan principle of 'one union in one plant for one grade of work'. We would not expect this principle to be promoted in a crude or inflexible way, and care would have to be taken to safeguard the wishes of workers themselves. Nevertheless, we are extremely concerned by the rash of small-scale quasi-professional

organisations that have developed recently claiming the right
to organise and represent sections of the white collar labour
force. If encouraged in an indiscriminating way they could
produce forms of union overlap and disputed jurisdiction that
will be extremely serious in five or ten years' time. The cause of
stable and effective representative negotiation is not served by
developments of this kind, and neither are the objectives of
industrial democracy and industrial peace.

But there are other aspects of the 1971 Act which will also
need to be changed in more drastic ways if our first objective is
to be realised. The most important of them are those provisions
which chapter Three argued are likely to discourage union
representatives from entering into detailed, comprehensive
agreements – especially those that force union leaders to choose
between the disavowal of lay representatives and various forms
of ignorance and hypocrisy about the exact nature of their
activities. This means revoking most of the Act's so-called
'inducement' liabilities and restoring most of the traditional
protections granted to trade unions in the context of trade
dispute under the 1906 Act. But more will be said about this
aspect of the Industrial Relations Act in the section below on
industrial sanctions.

Management's Role

On the employer's side the problem of stimulating and
developing effective negotiators takes a different form. Here it
is not simply a matter of encouraging the growth and extension
of representative collective institutions. Rather, it is a question
of encouraging the right kind of action within firms, particularly large firms. This means, above all, a commitment to the
right policies at the top and a willingness to allocate sufficient
resources to deal with them. Here it would help if there were a
change in company law designed to ensure that certain minimum responsibilities for the formulation of industrial relations
policy were laid on the Boards of companies. In the case of the
larger company these might include the requirement to appoint
at least one executive director and/or senior manager who would

be personally responsible for policy formation and its execution. A recent study of the problems of introducing bargaining reform in a number of companies gave very clear support to the view that it is important to ensure that the personnel function, in its widest sense, has a recognised place at senior decision-taking levels. This study showed that the development of long-term industrial relations policies or principles was more impressive and effective in those firms where the most senior full-time personnel manager was not too heavily involved in day-to-day problems and disputes.[2]

To supplement a policy of this kind, the existing procedure for registering collective agreements contained in the 1971 Act should be developed further. The Donovan Commission suggested there should be a statutory responsibility on companies of a certain size to register all their collective agreements with the Department of Employment. This was to be a speedy and compulsory process and had two objectives. First, 'to impress upon the boards of companies, and upon the public, that primary responsibility for the conduct of industrial relations ... lies with the board'. Second, ' ... to draw attention to those aspects of industrial relations ... which the public interest requires should be covered wherever possible by clear and firm company and factory agreements'.[3] We think the second aim is the most important, given the above proposals, but consider that the 1971 Act does not pursue it with sufficient vigour.

In the first place the effectiveness of the registration procedure has been considerably reduced because it has been run so far on a completely voluntary basis. Second, the whole process has lacked any sense of focus or selectivity. The task has been defined as one of literally recording the detail of procedures in their entirety, rather than in terms of defining and setting standards. The lesson to be drawn from this is that the registration of agreements should be undertaken by the National Mediation Board. The Board should be expected to develop criteria against which to judge the adequacy and extent of procedures reported to it. It should begin by focusing on particular aspects of agreements – such as those dealing with

Management by agreement

discipline, dismissals, redundancy and so on. The aim should be to evaluate what is registered against a particular model or series of models, along the lines of a more extended and detailed Code of Industrial Relations Practice. As in the case of the proposals of the Donovan Commission, and the provisions of the 1971 Act, there would be no sanctions beyond those required to enforce the act of registration. No employer would be required to enter into particular kinds of agreements, or penalised if he refused to do so.

Other Forms of Assistance

Finally, there are two other areas where it is arguable that legislative provisions of mutual advantage to both sides might contribute to the development of representative negotiators. One concerns increased public support for industrial relations training and an Industrial Relations Development Fund available to both employers and trade unions. In the area of public provision what is needed is an increased availability of industrial relations training courses at business schools and other educational institutions, as well as a general expansion of this area of training within the overall framework of training already provided under the auspices of the Industrial Training Boards. The kind of Development Fund required would make provision for financial assistance which extends beyond the proposals of *In Place of Strife*. On the trade union side, assistance would need to be provided for the expansion of training for union officials including shop stewards, the development of unions' often inadequate facilities and the employment of specialists. On the management side, again the emphasis would be on training, but there is also a need in the case of the small firm for assistance in the form of technical and specialist advice – i.e. the kinds of services at present provided by management consultants.

The last proposal to be advanced under this heading relates, once again, to the need to amend or reconstruct parts of the existing Industrial Relations Act. Here we refer to those parts of the Act dealing with the legal status of agreements. In chapter Four we sought to show why they were unlikely to help in the promotion of more comprehensive formal agreements, yet it must not be assumed from this that all forms of legally enforceable agreements should be prevented by law. On the contrary, where the parties to an agreement wish to enter into legal relationships the law should offer no barrier – as section 4(4) of the 1871 Trade Union Act did. It may be that in future individual employers and unions will come to welcome certain kinds of legal contract perhaps to symbolise their intention to move towards more permanent and stable relationships. For this reason, amongst others, we would favour a 'neutral' approach to legal enforcement. Collective agreements should be deemed to give rise to legal relationships if their form and content indicate that they are intended to do so. To avoid any confusion in this respect the law would insist on a suitable clause stating that this was so, as part of the preamble of any agreement claiming to have legal force.

Indirect Aids to Negotiation

We have considered so far those legal provisions that should help to promote the extension of systems of joint regulation based on collective bargaining. However, there is a form of representation that is not without its advocates whenever industrial relations reform is under discussion, which is not usually thought to be connected to collective bargaining as such. This is the notion of 'worker representatives' on management boards, either in private companies or in public corporations. Is there a case for legislation designed to stimulate this kind of development?

The answer must be brief; we would favour workers' representatives on management boards only in so far as they could be shown to be compatible with the extension of joint regulation by collective bargaining. Indeed proposals of this sort ought to be evaluated primarily in terms of their usefulness in this respect. Our argument throughout has been that the double challenge facing management can only be met by independent representative systems of negotiation. We have sought to show that this required clear lines of communication on both sides, and a respect for the very real differences of interest and function that exist between management and workers in both private and public industry.

For these reasons we would oppose rival systems of representation likely to cut across or undermine the development of strong and representative trade unionism; just as we would be against those that slur or disregard the ultimate responsibilities of management for the overall conduct of the enterprise. We also feel that once predictive bargaining and other forms of management by agreement are accepted and implemented, a form of workers participation will be operating that requires little or no supplementation. For all these reasons our approach to proposals for worker representatives on boards are tinged with scepticism and reservation. We are bound to regard them as, at best, second order proposals that fail to get to grips with the crucial problems as we see them.

Nevertheless, there are several reasons why all suggestions of this kind should not be dismissed out of hand. First, predictive bargaining and management by agreement are not yet in existence, and in many firms and industries it could take some time to produce significant moves in this direction. Second, there are now many countries – such as Germany, the Netherlands and Norway – where laws have existed for many years that result in worker representatives being placed on management boards. The effects of this legislation are complex and disputable, but few would argue that it never results in any extension of worker influence, or that such laws always work in ways that are inimicable to the growth of collective bargaining. Indeed many informed observers insist that they have been beneficial to both sides of industry, and to the community at large. Third, and partly because of this, several countries are proposing new experiments in this direction – notably Belgium and Luxembourg. Moreover, the European Economic Commission recently proposed an extension of such arrangements throughout the Community. It suggested that in all companies employing more than 500 people a minimum list of decisions should require approval by a specially constituted 'supervisory board', consisting of a minority of workers' representatives.

Such decisions would include those affecting the run down or closing of a plant, a significant limitation of expansion of its activities, and major changes in its organisation. As a member of the EEC Britain will be required to react to these proposals, and say how they might best fit our system of collective bargaining.

Our view is that there could be a place for a certain kind of worker representation in this country, so long as it is seen as primarily a supplement to the normal processes of collective bargaining. It could result in a form of shop-floor influence in areas normally beyond the reach of the bargaining process, and this could be mutually beneficial to both management and trade unions. Legislation of some kind would be necessary, if only because of the existing state of British company law. Without seeking to set out what would be required in detail, or deal with the host of practical problems, we would merely stress the need for four conditions to be met. First, the unions involved would have to invoke the provisions of such legislation; in effect they would ask to exercise their legal right to select and appoint board room representatives in firms of a certain size where they had obtained recognition. Second, the legislation would provide that the area of influence allotted to board room representatives would not cover those regulated by effective systems of collective bargaining – thus as bargaining developed, their role would tend to decline in importance. Third, within their prescribed areas, which might broadly follow the lines suggested by the EEC Commission, worker representatives would have to be accepted as 'spokesmen' or 'tribunes' of shop floor concerns and interests. In other words they would not be expected to take joint-responsibility for management decisions. Outside the sphere of collective bargaining these would remain a matter for management alone.

LEGAL SUPPORT FOR MEDIATION

Our second objective was related to the promotion of publicly-sponsored mediation services. Laws would be required for three main purposes: the provision of finance, methods of appointment, and powers.

Finance and Appointment

Finance would be provided by an annual grant to the national mediation board, which would assume overall financial responsibility for the work of area committees and specialist divisions. The full-time members of the Board would be formally government appointments, although it would be recognised that those chosen would have to command the respect of both sides of industry. At local level leading members of the industrial relations community would be asked to serve on area committees. They would be responsible for drawing up area panels of part-time arbitrators.

Functions and Powers

The terms of reference of the national mediation board should stress its independent position *vis-à-vis* the government of the day. It would also refer to the right of the board to determine most of its own case load, to initiate its own investigations and publish such reports as it considered appropriate. The right of access to information and (if necessary) the right to demand evidence from the parties should also be ensured. Aside from this, the mediation service would have no compulsory powers, except the right to refer certain kinds of disputes to a form of legally binding arbitration. But this aspect of mediation is more controversial and needs to be discussed separately.

The Case for Extending Ex Parte Arbitration

In chapter Seven a case was made for the development of arbitration on a voluntary basis. But it has also been made clear that legally binding arbitration will be required as a result of the proposals set out earlier in this chapter to deal with a range of specific functions; for example, disputes over the disclosure of information. For these purposes arbitration

would take a form resembling that presently provided by the
Industrial Arbitration Board, established under the 1971 Act.

However, an argument can also be made for the provision
of a slightly different kind of legally binding arbitration on a
more general basis. In practical terms this may be considered
in terms of the arguments for and against the reconstitution of
the Industrial Disputes Tribunal, whose operations were
described in chapter Six. It will be remembered that from
1951 to 1959 the IDT provided a form of arbitration that
could be unilaterally initiated by either side on a legally
enforceable basis. This type of *ex parte* arbitration was available
to deal with a wide range of issues including the settlement of
wage disputes. Both unions and employers had the right to ask
the Minister of Labour for a reference to the IDT without the
consent of the other party. Reference was at the discretion of
the Minister, but the award was legally binding on both parties
and became part of the individual worker's terms of employment. For most of its life the IDT was popular enough, but in
the mid-fifties the employers began to complain that its
awards were one-sided in their effects. By this they meant that
if a decision went against them they were bound to comply in
full and that was the end of the matter. On the other hand, it
was said, if a decision went against a union, things were not
that simple. First, union leaders could immediately decide to
put in a further claim demanding the balance of their original
demand. Second, the workers concerned could take what the
IDT offered and then strike for the rest. And even if the strike
was unofficial it might still be effective. In the end employers
could find themselves paying more than the IDT had awarded
in order to secure a return to work.

It should be pointed out that there was very little evidence
advanced to support these claims at the time. The Donovan
Commission found that virtually all IDT awards were honoured
by both sides. Strikes, even unofficial ones, were almost unheard
of. Nevertheless employers generally, and the CBI in particular, have remained opposed to the reconstitution of the
IDT in any form. For its part the TUC was originally against
the decision to abolish the IDT, and proposed the Tribunal's

re-establishment in its evidence to the Donovan Commission. However, in recent years there have been growing reservations about *ex-parte* arbitration amongst member unions. This is partly because the Industrial Relations Act has produced a reaction against all forms of legal intervention in collective bargaining, but also because of the growing suspicion of arbitration in general. In the public sector the fear has also been expressed that compulsory arbitration would be forced on the employers by the government whenever it looked as if the unions could achieve better results by militant strike action.

We remain in favour of the reintroduction of a form of *ex-parte* arbitration on the lines of the IDT, and think the danger of government intervention can be overcome by placing the machinery within the independent mediation services. There is no reason to suppose that if a new IDT was seen to be independent it would be ignored by workers whenever it appeared to grant them less than they demanded. Above all there is an increasing need for this kind of arbitration facility to deal with both disputes of right and disputes of interest in the years ahead. We are convinced that it could play a very useful role in the public sector. Yet we must recognise the strength of the opposition that exists to proposals to reintroduce a new version of the IDT in industry today. For this reason we would suggest a more limited initiative at the present time, which has been designed to try to overcome the stated objections of both sides, as far as this is possible.

The alternative we propose would give unions the sole right to set in motion the compulsory arbitration machinery. They would be able to ask for a reference to cover a defined bargaining unit, dealing with a given range of issues in dispute between them and an appropriate employer. Application would be made to the appropriate level of the mediation service, who would have the right to suggest to the parties alternative forms of mediation where appropriate. Awards made as a result of this procedure would become an implied term of the individual's contract of employment, thus binding the employer to observe them for a specified period of time. But, in deciding in the first instance whether or not to make an award, the arbitrators would have to take into account the assurances given to them by the unions. Unions would have to give an undertaking in advance to accept an award, and recommend it to their members as the full settlement of their claim. Otherwise the Tribunal would not make an award. If the union subsequently failed to honour such an undertaking, and encouraged some form of industrial action within a specified period to upset a decision of the arbitrators, then the procedure would not be made available to them again *for the same bargaining unit.* (At least this would not be allowed to happen for a considerable period of time.)

No doubt a proposal of this sort might still be objected to by those who oppose *all* forms of legally binding arbitration, on one ground or another, but it does at least deal with the stated objections of both sides to the operation of the former IDT. On the one hand the employers are not subjected to legally binding awards which unions are at liberty to ignore if they choose to do so. (At the most this can only happen on one occasion for any given bargaining unit.) Unions, on the other hand, could not be forced to accept legally binding arbitration whenever it suited employers, or the government of the day. Yet a procedure would have been established that could do much to promote the gradual acceptance of arbitration as the appropriate way of settling a wide variety of outstanding issues. And this would be a development of particular value in dealing with the problems of those groups for whom strike action is especially unsuitable or inappropriate. (For example agricultural workers, or teachers, whose conditions of work make it difficult for them to mount an effective strike. Or groups like nurses, probation officers or policemen, where strike action is more or less ruled out because its social consequences would be disastrous.) For groups like this unrestricted access to legally binding arbitration would provide an effective bargaining sanction for the first time.

But our hopes stretch still further. We favour an experiment on these lines because we believe that before long it would prove to be of considerable use to both sides of industry, and to the community in general. For we are convinced that in time many other groups would also come to regard such a procedure as appropriate to their situation – e.g. workers in vital public service industries, such as the railways, electricity and local government. We think the existence of this kind of arrangement would do far more than the emergency provisions of the Act to discourage damaging strikes in these areas. The trouble with the Act's emergency provisions (i.e. the compulsory cooling off periods and the strike ballot) is that they are only invoked by the authorities when they think that a strike is likely to be effective. In effect they are used as ways to give employers a breathing space – or at least this is how it looks to the workers. For this reason they are almost always resented, and tend to make a settlement more difficult to achieve. If one wants to find acceptable alternatives to industrial action they have to be seen to be less partial and discriminatory than this.

COMPREHENSIVE AND BALANCED INDUSTRIAL SANCTIONS

The case for comprehensive and balanced laws that regulate the use made of industrial power is a complex one that is seldom if ever fully developed. This is partly because arguments about the use of industrial sanctions, and their justifiability, are so often dominated by the case for and against the right of *workers* to withdraw their labour. At least the debate is conducted as if this were the sole or primary issue to be decided; as though trade unions and management had no particular interest in the form and content of the law in this area. Thus the implication is drawn that unions will naturally be able to exert sufficient influence over the content of collective bargaining wherever workers possess a well established and well developed right to strike. Similarly, the suggestion is made that the form taken by the right to strike will not affect management very much, so long as they retain their ultimate power to 'dispose of the capital of the business'. Thus a recent discussion of the legal limits of the right to strike in a number of countries including our own concluded that:

' . . . the imperative need for a social power countervailing that of property overshadows everything else. If the workers are not free by concerted action to withdraw their labour, their organisations do not wield credible social force. The power to withdraw their labour is for the workers what for management is its power to shut down production, to switch it to different purposes, to transfer it to different places. A legal system which suppresses the freedom to strike puts the workers at the mercy of their employers. This – in all its simplicity – is the essence of the matter.'[4]

There is much truth in this statement, but we would respectfully submit that things are not that simple. In fact trade union credibility and influence is not assured by simply ensuring the existence of a right to strike for workers as workers. These things depend even more on what the law says about the legal position of unions who seek to regulate and influence the use that is made of that right, and on how far laws are passed which help to structure and channel the use of the strike weapon through the medium of union membership and participation. And it has been one of the central arguments of this book that workers, management and even the community at large have an abiding interest in ensuring that this is the case. For unions are the only practical instrument which exists for structuring and focusing shop floor demands, so that they take the form of realisable and definable objectives.

But things are also rather more complex on the management side. Management interests are not sufficiently ensured simply because they remain free, in the last analysis, to abandon production, or to change its locale or end-product. For the most part if a management feels it must respond to the threat of strike action in this way it has already lost the battle. What management requires is a series of less draconic but more gradual sanctions – which would enable them to exert a range of industrial pressures on workers, while remaining in business. And here their legal right to discipline their own employees is a central requirement.

These considerations lead us to say that the kind of industrial

161

conflict laws we would like to see ought, above all, to fulfil two related objectives –

1 They should encourage the structuring of industrial action on the workers' side through union membership and participation in a way that maximises the opportunities for union leadership and influence, in conditions of union security and stability.
2 They should allow management to deploy an effective range of graduated sanctions on their side of the bargaining table, so that the collective power of the workers is in some way 'balanced' by a 'countervailing power' on the other side.

The rest of this section aims to suggest how these objectives might be achieved.

Union Leadership and Stability

It has already been argued how many of the provisions of the 1971 Act threaten union influence and stability by seeking to drive a wedge between a union's full-time officials, lay representatives and members. In particular it has been argued that the provisions that leave union leaders open to forms of non-contractual liability within the context of an industrial dispute, militate against the development and negotiation of more sophisticated forms of joint regulation. But the same arguments can be made against other types of 'inducement' liabilities – for example those that arise in relation to the so-called 'emergency' disputes. As we have seen all such provisions may end in the need to divorce the union and its leaders from the actions of the rank and file – e.g. through the process of withdrawing shop steward credentials, or taking disciplinary action against lay representatives and others. The logic of these provisions, for example in the docks, would have meant that in the recent containerisation disputes the Transport and General Workers' Union would have been forced to cancel the formal authority of a large number of accredited shop stewards, under pain of heavy fines, leaving the docks

without workgroup leaders of any importance with constitutional links with the major union involved. In effect the
law would have re-created one of the worst aspects of the pre-
Devlin situation in the docks, which the Devlin Committee
recognised as one of the main causes of extreme militancy and
disaffection in the industry.

This is not to say that the legal framework does not need to be
constructed in a way that facilitates the use of internal union
controls on workgroup behaviour – e.g. the use of the disciplinary provisions of union rule-books. On the contrary
unions must be allowed to retain reasonable disciplinary rules
that enable them to threaten with a range of penalties those
who refuse to abide by majority decisions.

But provisions of this kind are only likely to work if three
preconditions are censured. First, as the Donovan Commission
recognised, there must be a framework of joint-rules that is
designed to deal with actual problems, so that the unions can
expect their members to work within the established rules.
Second, the use of official union sanctions must be at the disposal
of the accredited union majority, as expressed through the
decision-making processes of the union (that is to say their
use must not be dictated by outside considerations – such as
the need to avoid the consequences of an action for inducement
of breach of contract). Third they must be allowed to operate
against a background of reasonable union security, where the
all-important disciplinary sanctions of the closed shop are once
more made fully lawful. For these reasons, and to avoid the
threats to union stability and bargaining structure they involve,
we would wish to see both the agency and closed shop provisions of the Act, together with its revocation procedures,
rescinded. As has been argued, in so far as they are effective
they are likely to undermine union security and prevent the
use of the disciplinary functions of the closed shop. They are
also apt to encourage the fragmentation of bargaining structure
and bargaining units, and the development of breakaway
trade unionism. Moreover they are designed to bring these
things about without even fulfilling one of the main stated
objectives – i.e. the protection of individuals against the abuse

of trade union power in the closed shop situation. (It is our view that more effective ways can be found to pursue this last objective within a legal framework that permits and even encourages union security arrangements. These ideas are discussed in the section below on individual rights.)

The Sanctions that Management Needs

It should be made clear at this point that the proposals advanced above are not suggested as part of a plea for placing trade unions 'beyond the reach of the law'. They are not seen as according unions a specially privileged legal status, which goes beyond that required to enable them to carry out their essential functions. Our point is merely that the legal history of trade unionism, from the time of Erle Commission to our own day, testifies to the fact that unions have to be given substantial degrees of legal protection if they are to develop as influential and stable organisations. Above all, union leaders of all kinds must be free to involve themselves in the decision-making processes of the shop floor without fear of the largely fortuitous consequences of random legal actions – initiated by individuals and groups who have failed to consider the consequences of their actions, in relation to either themselves or the community in general. Of course, given the fact that unions are in many ways unlike other associations – such as companies, or cricket clubs or professional bodies – the legal framework they need to carry out their functions will not look exactly like that required to suit the needs of these other bodies. But it does not follow from this that they enjoy unjustifiable privileges. Much of the argument of the traditionalists about the need to make trade unions conform to 'the same laws as the rest of us' is founded on this simple fallacy. What matters is not whether unions have legal privileges, but whether their privileges undermine and prevent the exercise of other types of civil rights that are equally important – for example the legal rights of management to deploy a range of effective industrial sanctions on their side of the bargaining table. We do not intend that the legal framework we are proposing would undermine the rights of management in this respect, although the point will perhaps become clearer after a short discussion of the basic needs of management in this area of the law.

In the first place management must retain the right to deploy the normal processes of industrial discipline in the course of an industrial dispute. This means, above all, that laws are required which safeguard their right to suspend or discharge on grounds of indiscipline, where the workers involved are contemplating or using various kinds of collective action. In the section below something is said about the need to ensure that management's right to dismiss is used within the context of a more extended law of unfair dismissal, but subject to these qualifications we would not advocate the circumscription or removal of such a right. Here we feel that the broad approach of the 1971 Act is correct. Section 26 of the Act specifically provides for lawful dismissal during and after a strike where participation in strike action is given as the reason. The only qualification is that the employer must treat all the workers involved in the strike in the same way. Similarly, Section 25 allows for dismissal as part of a 'lock-out'. We think the retention of such rights as these are part of the essential armoury of employers.

We also think employers must be allowed to suspend or dismiss workers who take industrial action in breach of their contract of employment – though it may be necessary to define more carefully what this means. It is also only reasonable to allow employers to include in the terms of contract an undertaking to observe established joint procedures for dealing with disputes, so long as the workers concerned agree to this. In this way strikes in breach of procedure become strikes in breach of the employment contract.

But management does not merely need rights against the workers it employs. It should be free to combine with other employers, as and when it wishes to do so. Indeed legal protection ought to be accorded to employers' associations on much the same basis as trade unions; their agents ought not to be liable to legal action when carrying out their essential functions, and if they wish to develop analogous practices to the trade union closed shop – as some of them do – these should be legalised as well. Employers should also retain the right to impose certain kinds of sanctions against trade unions as such, and here we feel that three very different kinds of rights are required.

The first is the right to implement management decisions once procedure has been exhausted. This means that a management which cannot get unions to agree on a proposed change should be free to impose this change unilaterally once the joint arrangements for seeking agreements have failed to produce a solution. In effect management gives notice that the modification in working arrangements which it favours will operate from a certain date – whether the unions like it or not. A declaration of this kind can be a powerful management weapon, and it is one of the most readily available in the management armoury. At the very least it prevents further prevarication and delay. It also presents the union with a significant challenge; either it must prepare for some form of collective action and the escalation of the dispute, or it must lower its sights and sue for peace. In effect management has called the union's bluff, if bluff it is.

Secondly, management must remain free to break off negotiations with the trade unions it recognises if it considers that this is tactically advisable in the course of a trade dispute. Thus the provisions we outlined earlier for encouraging the extension of collective bargaining by law should be viewed as techniques for developing general relationships. They are not ways of forcing employers to come to bargaining table whenever it suits trade unions. In other words, so long as an employer can show that he is normally prepared to bargain over wages, or discipline, he must be allowed the same right to stage tactical withdrawals as the unions he negotiates with. Not all proposals for extending bargaining rights by law make this point sufficiently clear.

Finally, as has been said, there should be no barriers to the development of legal obligations and liabilities between employers and unions, so long as it can be demonstrated that they were freely entered into on both sides. Employers should remain free to offer unions legally binding agreements, including agreements that contain financial penalties if they are broken. If unions can be persuaded to sign such agreements, by the prospect of better facilities, or improved conditions; this is a matter for them.

The aim of this section has been to indicate, in non-legal language, the broad outlines of a range of industrial sanctions that would safeguard the best interests of both sides when all attempts at mediation had failed. In general, the legal framework that is suggested closely resembles that advanced by the Donovan Commission. (Indeed, on most matters that are not specifically dealt with above it may be assumed that our views are broadly in line with those of the Commission – for example, we would not want to protect trade unions against actions in tort outside the context of a suitably defined 'industrial' and/or 'trade' dispute. Also we would not favour legalising picketing outside a person's home.) In the final section of this chapter more will be said about how these aims might be achieved by a simplification of existing legal terminology.

A FRAMEWORK OF INDIVIDUAL RIGHTS

Rights against Trade Unions

Some of the more important questions that remain to be discussed concern the position of union members, and would-be members, in closed shop situations. What is required is a way of combining lawful attempts to obtain and maintain union security with the fair and equitable treatment of the individuals affected. Once again our approach broadly follows that of the Donovan Commission – although we hope to improve on some of its specific proposals. Having reviewed the main arguments for and against the closed shop the Commission concluded that it was 'better to recognise that under proper safeguards a closed shop can serve a useful purpose and to devise alternative means of overcoming the

167

disadvantages which accompany it'.[5] The safeguards the Commission proposed dealt with the three main situations where abuse might occur:

1 Where workers with genuine conscientious objections are unjustifiably excluded from the job;
2 Where workers willing to join unions operating pre-entry closed shop are refused entry to them;
3 Where workers are unfairly expelled from unions operating closed shops and are subsequently excluded from the job on grounds of non-unionism.

In the first situation the Commission proposed a legal right to compensation to be paid by the employer. We think this is unfair where the employer can show that he has been prepared to meet demands for union security in a reasonable and civilised way, and that this aim could be best achieved by providing legal support for a form of union security arrangement which has been termed the 'registration shop'.

A registration shop differs from a closed shop in that it makes provisions for existing employees who are non-unionised at the time when the agreement is signed. Under its provisions an employer agrees to make trade union membership a condition of employment so far as existing union members and new entrants are concerned. In exchange for this the union agrees to allow existing employees, who have a genuine conscientious objection to joining the union, to remain at work. (In effect these employees are 'registered' at the time of the agreement as non-unionists.) This arrangement has the advantage of safe-guarding union security and stability while at the same time respecting the genuine convictions of established employees, who probably joined the firm when union membership was on a completely voluntary basis.

What we are suggesting is that unions seeking a registration shop agreement would be able to demand that their claim be investigated by the appropriate division of the mediation service. If the service found that the majority of workers con-cerned favoured this course, and that it was conducive to a stable bargaining structure in the industry or firm involved, they would recommend the negotiation of a registration shop agreement. (Legal sanctions to enforce such a recommendation against a reluctant employer would take a similar form to those in the 1971 Act designed to secure the implementation of agency shop recommendations by the present CIR.) Agreements suggested by the mediation service would provide for the registration and protection of conscientious objectors already employed within the specified area. Employers who could show that they were prepared to sign such agreements would be able to transfer their liability to unions or their members who took further action designed to force these people to leave the job. In these instances it would be possible for them to bring an action against the union or the workers involved.

Of course it will be necessary to ensure that the right to legal protection as a conscientious objector is not abused. It ought not to be a cover for those who merely wish to avoid paying union subscriptions, and for this reason conscientious objectors ought to be expected to pay equivalent dues to a nominated charity, as the 1971 Act provides. (To make this stipulation effective it should be lawful, in these circumstances, to deduct such dues from the pay packet of the workers concerned at source.) Also, it should not provide an under-cover base for dissidents, or breakaway trade unionists. For this reason it should be made clear that the rights of conscientious objection within the registration shop does not include the right to campaign against trade union membership in general. Fortunately, this is unlikely to be much of a problem. In our experience genuine conscientious objectors, who for the most part belong to minority religious sects, do not seek the right to urge others to follow their example. All they ask for is tolerance, and the registration shop is probably their best hope of achieving it.

The position of workers excluded from unions operating pre-entry closed shops is more easily dealt with, and again the Donovan approach provides a convenient starting point. The Commission did not want to prevent the use of the pre-entry closed shop for union security purposes, or to deny workers in casual trades a way of controlling entry to these trades. It also thought that workers should be allowed to refuse entry to their union to known dissidents; for example, those individuals who had been expelled previously for refusing to comply with union decisions. It also appreciated that unions confined to skilled workers ought to be allowed to refuse entry on the grounds that an applicant was not appropriately qualified. In short, the Commission wanted unions, in pre-entry shop situations and elsewhere, to retain the right to refuse entry in circumstances where it could be shown that this was not being done on 'arbitrary' or 'capricious' grounds; i.e. where the motive was the defence of group interests, applied in a consistent and impersonal way. This approach is the right one, but must include a positive declaration of the right of unions to refuse entry on these grounds. What Donovan suggested was a negative provision which merely provided that 'arbitrary' exclusion was to be unlawful in future. The 1971 Act follows this formulation to some extent, but could give rise to uncertainty and inconsistency in its legal interpretation.

The position of workers expelled from unions operating closed shops is more complex, if only because it raises the whole issue of how far the law should seek to regulate internal union behaviour in the interests of justice for existing members. Moreover, trade union attitudes to this problem have been affected by the controversy over the registration provisions in the Act.

For this reason a fresh approach is needed, which does not rely on the device of registration. The solution we would propose draws a distinction between the procedural and substantive aspects of the problem. On the procedural side the need is to ensure that when charges are preferred against an individual, particularly when those are likely to lead to expulsion in a closed shop situation, proper regard is paid to standards of 'natural justice'. Here the most effective safeguard is the right of the ordinary courts to declare an expulsion unlawful and to award compensation against the union where such principles are not observed. Fortunately, prior to the 1971 Act, the ordinary courts had developed an extensive area of jurisdiction in this field based on the practice of reading the principles of 'natural justice' into the rules of trade unions. So far as we know this practice was generally acceptable to trade unions. Certainly they did not refuse to appear before the courts involved. What is now needed is to develop this approach by providing that it should be administered, in the first instance, by partly lay tribunals where access is easy and cheap, and capable of dealing with cases promptly. There is also a case for spelling out the broad requirements of 'natural justice' in an enabling Act. But there is no need to insist on their embodiment in *existing* union rules as a pre-condition of registration.

On the substantive side rather more extensive provisions may be required. Here the crucial requirement would be to give the courts the power to review the relationship between a given offence and its penalty. They should be allowed to reduce or even quash those decisions they consider unduly harsh; for example, they could insist that expulsion was replaced by a small fine or a motion of censure. Once again these provisions could be made to apply to both registered and unregistered unions, and there would be no need to insist upon re-writing union rule-books to comply with a new set of 'model rules'. If necessary this procedure could be developed a stage further by laying down the grounds on which the courts could decide that punishment was unduly harsh. It could also be extended to include a right to consider complaints about elections and other democratic processes. Once again the trade union movement has not objected, in principle, in the past to the involvement of the law in this field, for example – the notorious ETU case in the 1950's. And again what is required can be achieved without the need for a registration procedure along the lines of the 1971 Act. Under our proposals the controversial but largely irrelevant device of registration can be effectively defused and relegated to its former relative unimportance; i.e. it can re-emerge as an uncontroversial administrative device which secures for those unions who want it, certain tax concessions on provident benefit funds. Indeed it may be that the best course would be to dispense with the provisions of registration altogether. There is in fact no good reason why tax concessions should not be made available to any organisation which satisfied the legal definition of a trade union. (The question of what should be included in the definition of a union for legal purposes is one we return to below.)

The legal regulation of internal union behaviour should be regarded as a last resort – required when there are inadequate or insufficient internal safeguards for members embodied in the union's own procedures and rules. For this reason where unions can demonstrate that they are applying the principles set out above they should be able to 'opt out' of legal regulation. A practical means of implementing this approach would be for the government to publish a list of the provisions they would like to see included in union rule books, covering such matters as the provision of natural justice, election practices, and so on. Included in the list should be a stipulation that disciplinary penalties should be referred to an independent review body with the power to quash or reduce them. Unions satisfying these requirements would then be allowed to opt out of the relevant provisions of the Act. That is, if a union made provision for an independent review body and agreed to abide by its decisions, as well as satisfying the other requirements in the list, the statutory tribunals would have no jurisdiction over the administration of its rule book and would have no power to consider individual appeals against the union. Similarly, in respect of its electoral procedures, if the standards laid down in the list were satisfied, then the ordinary courts would have no jurisdiction over this area of union government. It would then be possible for a union to formulate its own internal procedures and rules in such a way that there would be no need for any provision for appeal to an external legal body. This arrangement would apply so long as the national mediation board was satisfied with the workings of procedures.

In implementing these proposals an appropriate starting point would be to look at their feasibility in respect of TUC affiliates. The TUC could be asked to issue a set of model rules covering all these matters, and to establish its own independent review body. If these arrangements satisfied government requirements all TUC affiliates would be able to contract out of the statutory system, so long as they observed TUC model rules and practices. Such arrangements would have to be periodically reviewed, possibly on the basis of a government reference to the National Mediation Board.

Of course the TUC would not be the only organisation with the opportunity of opting out of the statutory provisions on behalf of its affiliates. Non-affiliated unions, and even TUC unions, could make their own arrangements if they wished. Nevertheless, for the great majority of unions an arrangement which allowed Congress to act as their agent in this capacity would offer the best way of reconciling legitimate demands for justice and equity for the individual member with the desire of trade unions for independence and flexibility in the administration of their own rules and procedures.

Rights Against Employers

The last part of the Act where substantive changes are required concerns the rights of individual workers against employers. Here those sections of the Act that relate to the notion of 'unfair dismissal' need examination. In this field the Act is a worthwhile step forward representing a considerable advance on the former common law position. Nevertheless, it has several weaknesses that need to be remedied.

First, it is arguable that compensation should be linked to the principle of a seniority right, as is the case with the Redundancy Payments Act, rather than based on the notion of 'probable loss'. Second, insufficient provision is made for re-employment or re-instatement. Third, although the Act provides for workers covered by a 'voluntary procedure' to be exempted from these provisions of the Act, such exemptions are not encouraged to a sufficient extent. Fourth, the coverage of the Act is far too limited; particularly in respect of the qualifying period of two years' continuous service with one employer.

On compensation we would favour an assessment which took into account length of service and the likelihood of future employment in an equally remunerative job. In re-employment and re-instatement it should be provided that those unfairly dismissed have a right to re-employment in similar work, and a right to re-instatement in their original job if an industrial tribunal considers this appropriate. Of course a worker should be allowed to waive his right to re-employment if he wishes, but re-entry to the firm ought not to be at the discretion of the employer, as it is under the present Act. Normally the Tribunal would be expected to offer to help provide an incentive for unions in this respect, only those voluntary procedures which applied to union members would be acceptable; although in these cases non-unionists would retain the right of access to voluntary procedures. Provision should also be made for a form of 'qualified exemption', where union and employers were allowed to 'contract in' to various parts of the statutory machinery – e.g. decisions requiring the award of compensation. In general, the mediation services would be asked to encourage and facilitate arrangements designed to promote all kinds of voluntary solutions where appropriate.

One of the most beneficial spin-offs from this approach would be a rapid extension of the coverage of the legal system, where it still applied. For as is well known the two-year qualifying rule was only chosen to reduce the level of the initial case load on industrial tribunals to manageable proportions. There are certainly no grounds for believing that unfair dismissal, as such, is less common during the first two years' service with an employer. Indeed, what evidence there is indicates that the reverse is the case. If the entire public sector were directed towards exemption, and unions and employers in the private sector were given sufficient inducement, a rapid reduction in the statutory case load would be feasible. Given this approach the qualifying period could be reduced to more reasonable proportions – say six months' service with one employer.

UNION SERVICES AND RESOURCES

This chapter has not attempted to deal with all the various provisions of the Industrial Relations Act, or with all industrial relations problems that might be assisted by changes in the law; e.g. the law relating to factory legislation, or the need to reform the operation of Wages Councils. On these and other matters there is only room at this point to stress that we would naturally favour the approach that did most to encourage the spread of systems of joint-regulation by union and employers.

However, there is one final issue of some importance that we would like to raise which relates to the level of union services to members and the way in which the law could help to promote their improvement. The framework of legal rights suggested for unions in this chapter is considerable; extended rights to organise and maintain contact with members to recognition, to disclosure and to arbitration; the right to operate closed shops and demand registration shops; rights of access to mediation services and development funds; protection against actions for inducement and so on. In our view these rights are both necessary and desirable so that unions are free to carry out their essential functions as the representatives and spokesmen of the challenge from below; helping to focus it on realisable and practicable objectives. The question is whether these rights will, in themselves, ensure that unions are actually prepared and equipped to fulfil this role. And if this is not the case, whether anything further can be done?

The main problem on the union side is clearly one of resources. For all kinds of reasons, largely associated with our system of industry-wide agreements, British unions have traditionally operated on the cheap. Thus there are fewer full-time officials per member in Britain than in any other comparable country. There are also far fewer educational facilities, training schemes, research workers and specialist services of all kinds. It is arguable that in the past this has not mattered too much, and even the Donovan Commission tended to take this view. But it is difficult to see how this view can be maintained today. As has been shown most of the new systems of plant and company bargaining make very considerable demands on union representatives, including shop stewards. They also require the use of more sophisticated bargaining techniques and considerable expert support on the

union side. More important still, their effective implementation
and review will necessitate a more developed and expensive
system of communication with the shop floor. And if bargaining
is to extend still further into the more complex aspects of
management decision-taking, say through the medium of
predictive bargaining, still more resources will be required.

Earlier in this chapter a case was made out for the provision
of external support for this purpose, say through the mediation
services development funds. But it must be realised that this is
not a complete answer, if only because many British unions will
be reluctant to apply for money of this sort, no matter how
independent its source may be. In any case it is much better if
unions take action on their own initiative to deal with the
resource problem by raising subscriptions. We think this is
possible and likely, given that one crucial limiting factor can be
overcome. This is the fear of union competition, especially
that insidious form of competition that derives from the appeal
of cut-price unionism. The fact is that there are in Britain
today too many unions who remain committed to the doctrine
of low subscriptions as a short-sighted recruitment tactic. If
others are to be encouraged to respond to what is involved in
the changes we want to see on their side of the bargaining
table there is a need for a simple and convenient method of
neutralising their fears in this respect. What is required is a way
of ensuring that as they come to appreciate the need to raise
their dues to meet future demands, they are not inhibited by
the fear of undercutting by rivals and would-be rivals.

A possible device that would ensure this would be to build a
minimum subscription rate into the legal definition of trade
unions. Organisations not charging at least this much would
not be classified as unions and would thus forfeit all the advantages and immunities that accrue from this status. Naturally
an initial subscription level would need to be agreed that
embraced all existing *bona fide* unions, but it would be possible
to make subsequent adjustments from time to time if undercutting was seen to be a barrier to further advance. If this
suggestion were adopted it should be combined with a similar
provision for 'opting out' as the one described above in respect

of union rules. In other words the TUC would be able to formulate its own 'voluntary' scheme involving a minimum subscription rate. If the government were satisfied that this was likely to be effective the legal regulation of subscription rates would not apply to TUC affiliates.

One of the most beneficial effects of a minimum subscription rate, built into the legal definition of a trade union, would be that it would kill off most forms of breakaway unionism at birth. Breakaways are almost always cut-price organisations, which grow and prosper largely because they promise to provide the same services for less money. Very few of them would survive for very long if they had to choose between a complete loss of their legal rights and a decent rate of subscriptions.

COMPREHENSIBLE LAWS

The fifth and final aim of an appropriate legal framework listed at the start of this chapter relates to the need to fashion legal provisions that the average person can understand. It might be argued that the case for this was self-evident on the grounds of simple justice – i.e. that people have a right to be able to understand the laws that apply to them in such a vital sphere as this – but we would not want to rest our argument solely on this point. The fact is that most trade unionists and managers, when they come into contact with the present complexities of the law, inevitably react with a mixture of contempt and bewilderment. They cannot believe that its tortuous by-ways and opaque ambiguities are necessary; unless, as they suspect, the whole thing is intended to confound them. Of course we realise that most lawyers are quite unable to accept that this is so, or agree that such an attitude is justified. We are convinced that they are wrong, and believe that the complexities and ambiguities of the law in this field are one reason why its provisions are so often ignored.

When the Industrial Relations Act was being framed this point of view often found expression in pronouncements of its sponsors (thus the Prime Minister promised an Act which would define worker-employer rights 'in plain English'). But as shown in chapter Four, in practice the Act has created more confusions than it has resolved – for example, in respect of the legal limits of the right to strike. Moreover, the conflicting interpretation by the NIRC and other levels of the judicial process has not always helped to make things clearer. Is there any way of ensuring that things are better arranged in future?

We think there is, if three problems are tackled. First, the Industrial Relations Act suffers from the defect that its provisions relating to many of the more important aspects of industrial action are scattered throughout 187 pages, 170 sections and 9 schedules. Thus the diligent layman who wants to know his rights in respect of the right to strike, or dismiss, or picket, has to trace his way through pages of close type to see if there is something there that applies. And for the most part, what he reads appears to be in no discernible order and to be made up of a series of different types of prohibition. To make matters worse if he consults a lawyer, he will be told that it does not always follow that the Act contains all he needs to know. There is always the possibility that common law liability will apply; for example, where a strike is called that is not covered by the definition of an industrial dispute provided in the Act.

But this is not the only difficulty. When he has extracted all the bits of the Act he needs, the diligent layman comes up against a further problem. For the most part the words used to describe both lawful and unlawful behaviour are not those he understands. There is, for example, no reference to 'blacking' in the Act, or 'working to rule', or an 'overtime ban'. What abounds throughout its pages are strange phrases like 'irregular industrial action' or 'action in contemplation or furtherance' or 'watching and besetting'. Even where familiar terms like 'strikes' or 'lockouts' are employed they are almost always associated with others that are not so familiar such as 'procurement' or 'inducement'.

Finally, and when these difficulties have been overcome, the diligent layman has to appreciate that the rights that result are for the most part indirectly stated. What emerges is either a series of negative prohibitions, such as the prohibition on action against extraneous parties, or immunities from specific civil wrongs like conspiracy. What is lacking are statements of positive rights of industrial action.

To remedy these defects we would advance three proposals. First a new Act should aim to bring together all the factors affecting important activities like the right to strike in one place. Those who read this part of the Act would be in a position to judge what were the relevant criteria in any case involving an allegation of unlawful strike action. Second, in prescribing and defining all legal rights and liabilities the new Act should employ ordinary terms and concepts wherever possible, avoiding an over-elaboration of types of prohibition. Of course these terms would have to be defined somewhere, in a precise and ambiguous way, and for this purpose some legal terminology would be needed. But even here, in our opinion, care should be taken to use relatively simple language, that is capable of being understood by an intelligent layman. Most important of all, perhaps, the practice of defining rights in negative terms should be abandoned – as is the case in most other countries. Instead the Act ought to spell out the positive limits of strike action, or the right to dismiss, or the right to participate in union activities. And it ought not to be necessary to know a great deal about the common law in order to be able to construe them.

It should perhaps be pointed out that what we suggest is not intended to undermine or get round the necessary role of the judiciary interpreting any Act. We realise that all Acts have to be interpreted. All we want is a way of formulating industrial rights that makes it more likely that they will be broadly understood and respected outside the ranks of the judiciary. This means that they must be written in as simple and straightforward a way as possible.

It would help to ensure that the role of the judiciary was exercised in a productive and flexible way if judges considering industrial law cases were accompanied by 'lay experts' of various kinds drawn from both sides of industry. Unfortunately this potentially progressive and useful idea has become a controversial one, largely because the National Industrial Relations Court was supposed to be established on these lines under the provisions of the 1971 Act. We can only hope that within the context of a less controversial Act it might be possible to return to the concept of 'mixed' courts of this kind, and that in this case members of the TUC might be persuaded to serve on the successor to the NIRC.

Notes

1 O. Kahn-Freund, *The Hamlyn Lectures: Labour and the Law*, Stevens, 1972, p. 3.
2 Department of Employment Manpower Papers No. 5, *The Reform of Collective Bargaining at Plant and Company Level*, HMSO, 1971.
3 Donovan Report, p. 47.
4 O. Kahn-Freund and Bob Hepple, *Laws against strikes*, Fabian research series 305, Fabian Society, 1972, p. 8.
5 Donovan Report, p. 163.

9. A programme for reform and its limits

'It is obvious, indeed, that no change of system or machinery can avert those causes of social *malaise* which consist in the egotism, greed, or quarrelsomeness of human nature. What it can do is to create an environment in which those are not the qualities which are encouraged. It cannot secure that men live up to their principles. What it can do is to establish their social order upon principles to which, if they please, they can live up and not live down.'

R. H. TAWNEY[1]

This chapter has two objectives. First, to summarise the proposals advanced in earlier chapters in the form of a practical programme for industrial relations reform. Second, to set this programme in a social and economic context; to show how progress in industrial relations is dependent on what is happening in the wider community that surrounds it.

A PROGRAMME FOR REFORM

1. *The rejection of authoritarianism*

Our central argument has been that the crucial problem of contemporary industrial relations derives from the difficulties that face management as a result of the interaction of two opposing pressures. The first of these we termed the 'challenge from within', since it is rooted inside the enterprise and derives from the demands and aspirations of those it employs. But this work-place based challenge reflects critical attitudes to authority, and rising expectations and standards, that are not confined to the work-place. It is expressed by an increasingly self-conscious and articulate workforce, seeking its rightful share

G

of power in industry. Its strength and pervasiveness provides an increasing opportunity and an expanding role for trade unionism.

Many managers share at least some of the attitudes and aspirations that have produced this challenge. Their problem is that they are also expected to grapple with the consequences of an equally pervasive challenge that is rooted outside the enterprise. This derives from a complex of factors, most notably those of increasing product competition, technological and business innovation, government policy and so on. In their effort to adapt the enterprise to meet the 'challenge from without', management finds it necessary to introduce an increasing rate of change within the enterprise, while increasing its overall efficiency. Yet somehow this must be done in a way that is compatible with the demands of the challenge from below.

Chapter Six demonstrated that this accommodation cannot be accomplished by a return to what we have called a traditionalist approach. The main defect of this approach is that it is rooted in out-dated and inappropriate authoritarian assumptions. Yet most managers know that an attempt to reintroduce authoritarian styles of management within the enterprise would result in fruitless confrontation. What is not so fully realised is that the problem also cannot be alleviated by an unrealistic faith in the early demise or gradual moderation of the challenge from within; whether this starts with the hope that unions will somehow disappear, or from the belief that legal regulations can transform them into 'responsible' organisations willing to 'restrain' the demands of their members. Such ideas assume that laws can transform the functions of trade unions, turning them into the aids of management and government; performing tasks that they appear to be unable to accomplish for themselves.

These notions are also fed by naïve and self-deluding myths about the relationship between union leaders and their members which we discussed in chapter Four. These only make sense if leaders are seen as the *agent provocateurs* of industrial conflict, habitually using their influence over members in an 'irresponsible' and 'coercive' way. These assumptions defy experience, and are not compatible with what is known and published about the nature of union leadership. They fail to appreciate its essentially consensual character, and its crucial role in focusing and structuring the challenge from below so that it takes a constructive and realisable form.

The only practical way of meeting the double challenge now facing modern management is by moving away from authoritarian responses towards an approach that is based on greater participation and consent. In practical terms this means extending and transforming the processes of collective bargaining, by introducing a system of joint decision-taking that we have termed *management by agreement*. This form of industrial self-government may be said to lay behind many of the proposals for collective bargaining reform first advanced by the Donovan Commission in 1968. (In chapter Five we described the strengths and weaknesses of the Commission's analysis, and sought to show how it could be developed to provide the basis for a more radical programme for reform.)

The tragedy has been that the years since the publication of the Commission's report have not been devoted to applying and developing its analysis. Instead, successive governments have sought to combine Donovan ideas with elements of a contradictory traditionalist approach. In chapters Three and Four we sought to show the consequences of trying to do this in the form of the 1971 Industrial Relations Act. We concluded that there was an inherent conflict between those parts of the Act designed to impose new legal liabilities on unions, and those sections intended to encourage a move towards more formal and precise agreements on the Donovan model. In so far as the former are used, or remain a credible threat, they are likely to produce a weakened union leadership, which is reluctant to enter into more formal agreements together with more fractionalised trade unionism. And even those parts of the Act designed to protect workers against the abuse of union power, are unlikely to have the desired effect, given the climate of uncertainty and insecurity it has already encouraged.

All this is not to suggest that other parts of the Act will not be beneficial. It is not to deny that one of its most desirable effects so far has been to focus the attention of top management on the need to have a policy for industrial relations. We have not argued that no benefits can possibly come from the Act. Our position is that the good that results is sometimes fortuitous, often achieved in spite of its other intentions, and that more progress could be made more easily if the Act were purged of its counter-productive traditionalist objectives.

2. *The acceptance of management by agreement*

In chapter Six we, described the outlines of an alternative approach. This involves an acceptance by management of the need to extend joint decision-taking within the enterprise. It will mean abandoning traditional employer beliefs about sacred subjects, or reserved areas of decision-making, that must always remain beyond union influence. Unions must be granted the right to seek to influence management policy in *any* area that affects their members, if possible by signing collective agreements that regulate and determine how management will act in future.

But the notion of management by agreement does not mean that attempts to widen the area of joint agreement will always succeed. Management is not bound to agree with the unions on the pace of expansion, or the need to avoid a shut-down. Unions will not be given a veto power over management appointments, or promotion policies. Disagreement will continue to be rooted in real conflicts of interest which we would not wish to deny. What this approach does offer, however, is the possibility of a wider framework of agreement, plus a forum within which the demands and aspirations of the shop floor can be directly related to the exigencies and pressures that play upon the enterprise. The problems posed by developments in the economic and technological environment of the firm thus become matters of common concern to both sides, to be dealt with jointly through the bargaining process.

Of course this involves major changes in bargaining policy and behaviour on both sides which we outline in some detail in the latter part of chapter Six. On the management side additional resources and expertise will be required, plus a willingness

to initiate moves towards fixed-term agreements that express an
'open-ended' approach. Management will also have to be
willing to act more consistently; it will have to learn to give its
reasons and to argue out its position in ways that may seem
time-wasting.

But much will be expected from unions as well. Successful
moves towards management by agreement will undermine their
freedom to react to the day-to-day pressures coming from below.
Bargaining will be more 'structured' and the introduction of
fixed term agreements will mean that there will be a 'closed
season' for demands against the enterprise. As the area of joint
control extends unilateral customs and practices that are well
established on the shop floor will need to be modified. Unions
will have to explain to their members why this should be so,
and gain their agreement. To do this they will require more
sophisticated and developed systems of communication, participation and additional resources.

In the last part of chapter Six a new form of collective bargaining designed to further management by agreement in a
precise and detailed way was described. This will involve a shift
away from inquisitions into past grievances and claims, towards
future initiatives and problems that need to be jointly solved.
The agreements resulting from such a process would be jointly
implemented and monitored and thereby provide the basis for
subsequent negotiations and agreements. They would also provide a suitable context within which to explore a whole range of
decision-taking experiments, including more autonomous systems of work and new methods of stimulating involvement
and participation on the shop floor. We have called this kind of
joint decision-taking predictive bargaining.

What is proposed is not a system of workers' control, but it is
the most meaningful way of promoting the aims of workers'
participation in management and the ideals of industrial
democracy. Because it is based on the extension and transformation of established systems of collective bargaining it is compatible with the maintenance of strong, independent and
representative trade unions, ready and able to disagree with
management if and when this is necessary to preserve their

independence and serve the interests of their members. It also does not seek to slur over or disregard the ultimate responsibilities of management for the overall conduct of the enterprise.

Because these aspects of collective bargaining are essential, and reflect real differences of interest between management and the managed, we would not favour systems of worker-representation that are likely to cut across them. For these reasons our approach to proposals for the direct representation of workers on the boards of companies are tinged with scepticism and reservation. Nevertheless properly controlled schemes of this kind can make some contribution to the problem of how to extend shop floor influence in areas not easily covered by collective bargaining. Consequently, at the end of chapter Six, we point out how this might be done.

3. *The promotion of constructive mediation*

All forms of bargaining reform require a commitment from the parties themselves if they are to produce results. Moves in the direction of management by agreement could be initiated by any management that felt it was likely to awake a suitable response from the unions it deals with. But in chapter Seven it was argued that the kinds of reforms we wish to see are unlikely to be introduced at a sufficient pace and on a sufficient scale without outside help and assistance. Partly because in many firms where radical changes are most desirable the pressures of the existing situation make it difficult to believe that time and resources will be found on a sufficient scale. While in others, where day-to-day problems are not so pressing, there may not be a sufficient sense of urgency. Because of these considerations the promotion of systems of management by agreement will require the active involvement of government. For this reason we have proposed supplementing the influence of education and example with a network of institutional arrangements and a legal framework which will stimulate and encourage the process of reform. At the centre of these proposals are our suggestions for a range of independent mediation services, publicly financed and supported, but outside the day-to-day control of government.

The aim would be to provide a powerful catalyst for change and an influential instrument for promoting industrial peace. Both functions are required since even in its most developed forms, collective bargaining cannot be expected to dispose of all disagreements. One of our main criticisms of the Donovan Commission was that they failed to provide any effective short-run proposals for dealing with the rising tide of industrial unrest in Britain which was already apparent when they were writing. (In many ways this has become an even greater problem since.) It was partly for this reason that their excellent case for concentrating on long-term bargaining reform failed to discredit the much less plausible case of the traditionalists which focused on laws designed to curb trade union power.

Instruments of constructive mediation offer a more promising way of dealing with both short- and long-term problems. For mediation is a method of resolving or avoiding industrial disputes which concentrates on ways of discovering more acceptable solutions other than strike action. By contrast all attempts to weaken the position of one of the parties can only hope to suppress the symptoms of disagreement. In themselves they can solve no disputes. And on the record of the Act so far they are just as likely to inflame others.

What is needed is a range of interrelated and independent agencies, designed to encourage both strategical mediation (i.e. the long-run reform of the bargaining system in the direction of management by agreement) and tactical mediation (i.e. conciliation arbitration and inquiry as a means of avoiding or resolving immediate disputes). In chapter Seven we also demonstrated how the existing range of services provided by the Department of Employment failed to provide what was required. A detailed case was made out for a new and different organisational structure, which would operate in a much more interventionalist way and exercise a more pervasive influence. It should be designed to promote four main objectives:

1 The maximum involvement of serving trade unionists and practising managers in the overall administration of the service;

2 The development of a full-time staff of mediation officers, based on local communities and serving their needs;
3 A policy of developing the workload of the services through industrial contacts, especially at shop-floor level;
4 The encouragement of interrelated types of services; designed to stress the connection between tactical and strategical mediation.

To gain the full benefit from a service of this kind, management and trade unions will have to agree to serve on the proposed Area Mediation Committees and a National Mediation Board. They will also be encouraged to second some of their staff to play a full-time role in day-to-day administration of the agencies. Government, for its part, will have to accept that the services provided could not be withdrawn, or manipulated, to meet its own short-run interests. Above all government must accept that public mediation facilities could no longer be used as a 'back door' way of seeking to influence the pattern of wage settlements.

Fortunately, as seen in chapter Seven, this use of conciliation, arbitration and inquiry has always been counter-productive. It undermines the acceptability of all forms of mediation without making any contribution to the fight against inflation. It is based on the implausible contention that settlements arrived at through the intervention of mediation are normally above levels set by the parties themselves as a result of direct negotiation. What evidence there is, is against this assumption, and there are good reasons why this should be so.

The chances are that the fight against inflation in recent years has been seriously harmed by the attempts of successive governments to misuse established mediation services in the mistaken interests of incomes policy. Such actions always strike workers as unfair, and they are right to feel as they do. In this way they destroy support for the very notion of incomes restraint, which must be approached by means of a quite different framework of institutional arrangements that are designed to exercise an equal degree of influence over the totality of factors that contribute towards rising prices.

Once government overcomes these and other mistaken fears about the extended use of mediation it can then make a major contribution to the solution of all kinds of industrial relations problems. To help to give concrete expression to these claims chapter Seven ended with a number of examples. The first two involved the use of constructive mediation to solve a recognition dispute and improve industrial relations in a strike-prone firm. The last three involved raising productivity in the Health Service, a new system of collective bargaining in the construction industry, and an account of how our proposals might have prevented the recent wave of industrial unrest in the docks.

4. *An appropriate legal framework*

Suitable laws to promote the aims of management by agreement and constructive mediation will be needed to achieve the following six objectives:

1 *Representative negotiators on both sides of the bargaining table, able and willing to enter into agreements leading to a greater degree of joint control over management decisions*

On the workers' side this aim requires two critical forms of legal support for trade unions; the *right to combine* and the *right to representation*. The first means that employers must not be free to dismiss or discriminate on grounds of membership of or participation in an independent organisation of workers. The second involves the right to a form of legally binding arbitration where employers are refusing to grant recognition to an appropriate union.

What we would propose in both these respects does not differ very much from what is contained in the present Act, although we would not confine these rights to registered unions and their members. What must be noted, however, is that for us recognition is a much more far-reaching concept. We would regard any attempt by unions to shift forward the frontier of joint-regulation as a recognition issue. A claim for recognition arises when management refuses to accept the union's right to bargain over any aspect of management decision-taking. Thus unions recognised for the purpose of wage bargaining, or redundancy issues, can still claim the right to be recognised for the purpose of participating in productive bargaining. But they would have to demonstrate their own willingness to take this form of bargaining seriously. Once this has been established the same procedure would be available to them to force management to the bargaining table. And a similar procedure would be there for use against employers who refused to disclose relevant information during the course of such bargaining. In this way the law would assist the extension of joint rule-making in a far more ambitious and far-reaching way than that contained in the 1971 Act.

On the management side a change in company law is needed which makes boards of companies directly responsible for the conduct of industrial relations, including a requirement that at least one executive director and/or senior manager should be appointed with sole responsibility for the development and execution of policy in this area. The National Mediation Board must be charged with the task of registering agreements, and developing criteria against which to judge their adequacy.

Other forms of assisting the development of representative negotiators should include more support for industrial relations training and a move towards a more 'neutral' approach on the question of the legal enforceability of agreements. The law should prevent no barrier to legally enforceable agreements, as has normally been the case in other countries with a different tradition to ours. Much of the traditionalist case has been based on the mistaken belief that what others were free to do if they desired we could be made to do by law. To see through this fallacy is not to deny the role that might be played by the establishment of legal relationships, if this is what the parties want.

2 *A network of mediation services, exercising an increasing influence on the process of bargaining reform and the resolution of industrial disputes*

Legislation would be required to provide finance, specify functions and guarantee independence. It would also be necessary to provide a novel form of *ex parte* arbitration. Unions who wished to do so, should be able to refer disputes to independent mediation, including a form of legally binding arbitration. Awards made as a result of this procedure would become an implied term of the individual's contract of employment, thus binding the employer to observe them for a specified period of time. To take advantage of this procedure unions would have to give an undertaking in advance to accept the award and recommend it to their members. If they subsequently failed to honour such an undertaking, and encouraged industrial action, the procedure would not be made available to them again for the same group of workers. Once established a procedure of this sort should lead to the gradual acceptance of more peaceful ways of settling disputes, especially those in the public sector where their consequences are apt to be socially disastrous – i.e. on the railways, in electricity supply or local government.

3 *A comprehensive range of industrial sanctions, available to both sides when there is failure to agree*

Laws are required to fulfil two objectives. First, to encourage the structuring of industrial action on the workers' side through union membership and participation in ways that maximise the opportunities for union leadership and influence in conditions of security and stability. To this end the inducement liabilities of the 1971 Act must be set aside, together with those parts that prevent effective union security agreements and stimulate the fragmentation of bargaining structures and the growth of multi-unionism. As a result union leaders and unions would no longer need to divorce themselves from their members to protect their position. They would also be free to use the entry-control and disciplinary functions of the closed shop.

Secondly, such rights would need to be complemented by similarly effective ones on the management side, so that the collective power of the workers is complemented and balanced by a countervailing power. Employers must be allowed to suspend or dismiss on grounds of industrial misconduct, subject to the qualification that they treat all workers alike in the context of a trade dispute. Dismissal for breach of contract should also be allowed and employers should be free to combine with other employers, and use analogous practices to the closed shop if they wished to do so. They must remain free to implement management decisions when procedure is exhausted, and have the right to break off negotiations with trade unions on tactical grounds. These rights are far more important to employers than the doubtful right to exploit the liabilities of unions under the 1971 Act.

4 *The rights of workers against unions and management*

In the case of genuine conscientious objectors who face exclusion from the job because they will not join a union operating a closed shop, our proposals involve the legislation and promotion of a form of union registration agreement known as the *registration shop*. This protects the rights of established employees with genuine conscientious objections, while offering the union an effective security arrangement.

The position of workers excluded from unions operating preentry closed shops can be dealt with along the lines of the 1971 Act, so long as the legitimate grounds of exclusion are specified by law. To deal with workers unfairly expelled from unions in closed shop situations we propose drawing a distinction between the procedural and substantive aspects of the problem. This would provide the basis for a more effective protection of minorities than is contained in the 1971 Act. Yet it would enable us to dispense with the need to insist on the registration of unions, as a condition of legal protection. This has turned out to be an unnecessarily divisive and controversial device.

Our proposals would mean that in dealing with expulsion cases unions would have to observe the principles of natural justice, and even then the penalties they imposed would be subject to judicial review. Yet it would be possible for them to opt out of these regulations if they could show that they were willing to embody them in their own rules.

In the case of rights against the employer we would favour changes in the law of unfair dismissal. There should be higher levels of compensation, provision for reinstatement and reemployment, and more effective ways of developing voluntary procedures which would relieve the burden on the courts and enable the qualifying period of the Act to be reduced.

5 *The improvement of union services and resources*

It was argued in chapter Eight that if unions were to be given a broad framework of rights to enable them to play their full part in developing a system of management by agreement, it was reasonable to ask whether the law could do anything to make it more likely that they would prepare themselves for this task. The main problem here is one of resources. Largely for reasons outside their control British unions have traditionally operated on the cheap. Because this tradition now needs to be broken, and fear of competition in the form of cut-price trade unionism is an important limiting factor, we proposed that a minimum subscription rate should be built into the legal definition of a trade union. An opting out arrangement would be possible in the case of TUC affiliates and others who could show that they were operating a voluntary scheme to secure the same effect.

6 *The formulation of legal rights and obligations in a form that is comprehensible at the work-place*

A new industrial framework that is likely to be observed and respected must be capable of being understood by those it is supposed to influence. One way of helping to secure this aim would be to bring together all the factors affecting important aspects of the law, such as the right to strike, in one section or part of a new Act. Another aid would be to ensure that, wherever possible, ordinary terms were used to describe every-day industrial events – such as strike action, picketing and so on. Finally, statements of legal rights and privileges should be couched in a positive form, replacing the traditionally negative description of immunities and liabilities. Laws in this field should be administered and interpreted by courts and tribunals including lay representatives drawn from both sides of industry. The unsatisfactory and unfortunate example of the National Industrial Relations Court ought not to prejudice the proper use of this kind of arrangement.

5. *The time scale of reform*

The programme advanced above cannot be realised overnight; its maximum impact may not be felt for some years. Yet there can be no doubt what is needed now to give it an immediate impetus: a government which is prepared to make a permanent break with a partisan policy in mediation and willing to introduce a new industrial relations Act that finally repudiates traditionalist authoritarian assumptions. So far no government has been prepared to go this far, and the present government may well feel that a *volte face* on this scale is quite out of the question – at least for the time being. Does this mean that in the interim nothing can be done?

Fortunately this is not the case. Participative solutions to industrial relations problems are not entirely dependent on the prior existence of a satisfactory legal framework. More sensible and rational systems of collective bargaining can be agreed without the aid of independent mediation. Indeed, it has been an essential part of our argument that this is already taking place at the present time. In this sense there is nothing new about the idea of management by agreement. Even the notion of predictive bargaining is a development and extension of bargaining experiments that are already in existence or in the process of negotiation. Developments of this sort will continue, irrespective of what government may or may not do. This book was partly stimulated by their growth, and by a desire to see them extended.

Nevertheless, our argument has been that while certain parts of the Act remain there will be a continuing threat to reform. The general atmosphere of industrial relations will continue to be threatened by the possibility of ill-judged but well-publicised attempts to invoke the provisions of the Act against union leaders. Threats of fines and sequestration will continue to place officials and shop stewards in a difficult position when seeking to carry out the wishes of their members. Union officials will continue to be faced with the series of unsatisfactory choices outlined in chapter Four, and as a result will not be able to play their full part in developing the right kind of leadership.

It follows that those who really believe in bargaining reform, and understand what it involves for trade unions, must continue to make the case for a modification of these parts of the Act as a first priority. And once this step is taken it will be easier to make the case for further reforms – for example, the restoration of the legality of the closed shop.

INDUSTRIAL RELATIONS REFORM AND ITS LIMITS

Throughout this book we have criticised both the traditionalist standpoint and the Donovan diagnosis, but usually from rather different points of view. This final section makes one final criticism of both approaches, based upon a common defect. Both tend to assume that industrial relations problems can be dealt with more or less in isolation. Both could be said to be too narrow in the scope of their analysis and the extent of their prescriptions. In the case of the Act, traditionalist ideas suggest that legal liabilities fastened on unions and union leaders can transform established patterns of shop floor behaviour. In the case of the Donovan Commission the implication is that new procedures, or better agreements, are all that are required to tackle the problem of strikes, labour utilisation and wage drift. In each case, progress is to be brought about by compulsions or initiatives designed to make a direct impact on the industrial relations system itself. It is time to correct this impression, and emphasise how far the industrial relations system is what sociologists would term a 'sub-system'. This means that it can be crucially affected by economic, social and political events that are beyond the control of those who sit round the bargaining table.

The most obvious example of this relationship concerns the connection between industrial relations problems and the overall level of management efficiency. If payment systems degenerate and produce inequities, the roots of the problem are often to be found in the work-study department. If labour is badly used, and unnecessary overtime develops, it is almost always partly the result of inadequate supervision. If workers have to be laid off, or plants have to be closed down, the reasons usually include failures of research and development, or mistakes in marketing strategy. Certainly if anything is to be done to deal with these problems there is almost always a need to do something about other aspects of the business.

But even the most efficient and well-intentioned of managements may be powerless in the face of changes in the economic environment. These may produce a sharp decline in the product market, or a prolonged period of stagnation. They could result in constant variations in demand, coupled with an increase in effective competition. All such developments will influence the general climate of industrial relations, for they will affect take-home pay, or the level of overtime, or the amount of casual labour that is required. In extreme cases they may make large-scale redundancy unavoidable.

But of course the state of the product market for a particular firm or industry is affected by the overall level of demand in the economy. And this in turn is influenced by the ability of the economy to sustain a relatively high level of economic growth. And all these factors have an impact on the state of industrial relations if only because they are known to have an influence on the level of employment and the prospects for future employment. Where employment prospects are high, and there is some prospect of redeployment, management finds it much easier to get union representatives to think in terms of the need to help the firm to adapt to long-term requirements. Where this is not the case, union horizons tend to narrow; officials are forced to focus on the immediate sectional interests of threatened groups within their membership. In this kind of atmosphere all proposals for change awake the maximum resistance on the union side. It becomes much more difficult to gain agreement for the internal changes that are needed to adjust to the challenge from without.

These facts are stressed for two reasons. First, to avoid appearing to commit the errors of others, who have assumed that their prescriptions, or preferred institutional frameworks for industrial relations are likely to provide permanent and lasting solutions. Second, to emphasise once again the crucial role to be played by government in making change possible. In their case commitment to management by agreement and constructive mediation is not enough: a government that wishes to be taken seriously about industrial relations reform must also demonstrate that it is able and willing to take action to create the kind of general climate within which initiatives in the direction of reform are likely to work. And this may prove to be a more difficult task than any allotted them so far.

The concrete examples in chapter Seven indicate what might be required in particular instances – for example, an extension of public ownership in the docks, a system of decasualisation and licensing in construction, and the reform of the rating system in local government. Others could be added, but at the moment we are suggesting much wider and more general assistance.

A few illustrations of what we have in mind are in order, although they can only be dealt with briefly. For example, we think it would help if industrial relations reform takes place against the general background of a much more active manpower policy – say on the Swedish model.[2] This would involve establishing a much firmer link between the public employment service and existing arrangements for training and retraining. It would also require a very considerable increase in Government Training Centres, a new system of training levies and the creation of a powerful National Manpower Board. So far no government in Britain has taken this area of policy sufficiently seriously, and none has been prepared to make adequate resources available.

Then again, we think there is a need for a more interventionist policy in relation to regional development, especially one that focuses much more directly on stimulating employment in development districts. (A policy of this kind might well involve a regional pay-roll subsidy.) New public instruments might also be required to stimulate the flow of investment in a more employment-creating way – such as those pioneered in Italy and elsewhere.[3]

But a government that wishes to be thought to take industrial relations reform seriously must also try to avoid forms of incomes policy that focus almost exclusively on trade union members, especially those which rely on the abuse of mediation, and attempts to persuade employers to stand up to union demands. Conversely, it would help if any government can gain agreement for a more broadly based prices and incomes policy, which stimulates the reform of pay differentials in a more rational and far-sighted way. But to achieve this it may be necessary to develop other policy objectives and instruments – including statutory price controls and measures designed to restrain non-unionist incomes. Finally, the ideas of social planning and industrial democracy, that inform and underlie the notion of management by agreement, are related to more general aims and aspirations that extend beyond the workplace. The emphasis on the long-run that is implicit in the notion of predictive bargaining will not be helped by a government whose own economic policy lurches from crisis to crisis. A government which is urging democracy on others ought to appear to be interested in democracy itself.

It will not be easy for any government to promote these and similar objectives, even if some of them do not run contrary to its deepest convictions. Nor will they be culpable if they fail, any more than managers or trade unionists. Rather, what government must do is to demonstrate that they are at least aware of the connection between industrial relations reform and their other policies. They should not appear resentful, or even surprised, when told that what they felt they must do to safeguard the currency, reduce taxation, fulfil their treaty obligations, or secure votes, has set back the course of industrial relations reform. At least it should look as if they were aware that this might happen, and that they have counted the cost of their actions.

However, this does not imply that industrial relations reform is so difficult that it is hardly worth while attempting. In any case modern management must try to find some way of accommodating to the twin challenge that it faces, if the business is to grow and prosper, or even survive. And for unions and their members accommodation is hardly less important, for they have at least as much to lose. In the case of the government, and the community at large, success in this area may truly be said to hold the key to progress in other important fields – not least the restoration of Britain's 'competitive edge'.

Like all worthwhile objectives reform in industrial relations is often elusive and sometimes transitory. Its pursuit requires that mixture of patience and persistence that is always in short supply. We have sought to show that there is no other alternative. The thing to do is to simply try.

Notes

1 R. H. Tawney, *The Acquisitive Society*, Fontana, 1961, p. 176.
2 For an up-to-date account of Swedish Labour market policy see Santosh Mukherjee, *Making Labour Markets Work*, PEP, 1972.
3 For a recent study of the Italian Institute for Industrial Reconstruction see Stuart Holland (Ed), *The State as Entrepreneur*, Weidenfeld and Nicolson, 1972.

Index

Index

Closed shop *(cont.)*
  Industrial Relations Act 46–50, 65–73, 163–4
  post-entry 67–9, 163
  pre-entry 46–7
  See also Agency shop; approved closed shop; 'Registration shop'
Coal industry 126
Code of Practice: See *Industrial Relations Code of Practice*
Collective agreements 152–3, 190
  fixed term 41, 106, 109
  Industrial Relations Act 42–5, 60–5
  legal enforceability 16, 25, 42–5, 60–5
Commission on Industrial Relations 78, 117, 131, 146–7, 169
  Donovan Report 27
  In Place of Strife 34
  Industrial Relations Act 37, 44, 48–50, 63, 70–1
  strategical mediation 120–1
  TUC 132
Committees of Investigation 116, 117, 120, 123
Committees of Settlement 117
Conciliation
  CBI–TUC Service 129, 141
  neutrality, principle of 121–9
  unconstitutional strikes 118
  unofficial strikes 118
  voluntarism, principle of 117–18
Conciliation Act (1896) 117, 121
Confederation of British Industry 129, 132, 141, 157
Conservative Party 2, 10, 11, 14, 34
  See also A Giant's Strength; *Fair Deal at Work*: Inns of Court Conservative and Unionist Society; *Trade Unions for Tomorrow*
Constructive mediation 6, 113–43, 186–9
Contract of employment 15, 165
Courts of Inquiry, 116, 117, 120, 123, 125, 126
Covent Garden 9

Department of Employment:
  arbitration 117, 119, 157
  Conciliation Service 117–19, 122–3, 126, 129–31, 134
  Donovan Report 27
  Manpower Advisory Service 117

202

Index